Natural Gas Trading in North America

Richard Lassander

and

Glen Swindle

First published in 2018

First Edition

Visit our website at www.scovilleriskpartners.com

Scoville Risk Partners
101 Carnegie Center
Suite 100
Princeton, NJ 08540

Library in Congress Cataloging-in-Publication Data
Lassander, Richard
Swindle, Glen

Natural Gas Trading in North America
ISBN 978-1-7322382-0-6

Cover photo: CanStockPhoto.com

Contents

PART I
Overview

Natural Gas Trading in North America

NATURAL GAS TRADING IN NORTH AMERICA presents the core knowledge required to work on a natural gas trading desk in North America. The material surveyed spans historical market context, fundamental drivers and the mechanics and instruments used to trade and risk manage a natural gas portfolio. This book is intended to be accessible to a broad array of readers, from those trading markets directly, to origination, structuring and control groups, as well as those working in investment banking and project development for whom an understanding of how the markets are traded is essential in their daily activities.

Glen Swindle has held senior positions at Constellation Energy, where he ran the Strategies Group for the merchant energy business, and at Credit Suisse, where, as Managing Director and Co-Head of Power and Natural Gas Trading, he ran structured trading teams responsible for significant aspects of the North American energy business. Previously he held tenured positions at UCSB and Cornell University, as well as an adjunct faculty position at New York University where he lectured extensively on energy valuation and portfolio management. He is also on the Energy Oversight Committee for GARP's Energy Risk Professional Program and is a frequent speaker at panel discussions and webinars. He is the author of Valuation and Risk Management in Energy Markets (Cambridge University Press, 2014). Glen holds a Ph.D. in Applied Mathematics from Cornell University, an M.S.E. in Mechanical Aerospace Engineering from Princeton, and a B.S. in Mechanical Engineering from Caltech.

Richard Lassander has over 20 years' experience of the energy markets from Enron, to various hedge funds and later to Credit Suisse, where he ran the Northeast Natural Gas Trading Desk. Richard was also the head of Fuel Trading at Cogentrix for their merchant generation fleet. He holds a M.S. in Accounting from CUNY, Baruch College, a B.S. in Finance and a B.S. in Economics from Louisiana State University.

Preface

THERE IS AN element of trepidation when you first set foot on a trading floor as a participant. Not only do you realize that the economic stakes can be high and bad decisions irreversible, but you also anticipate that there will be a lot of things that you simply do not know—from the arcane knowledge and vernacular of the particular markets in which you will be involved, to the unusual culture and vibe of trading desks.

Whether you are fresh out of college or a seasoned researcher or academic, during the first days and weeks you find yourself searching for materials that can help you learn what you need to know to function in your new environment and to generally avoid embarrassing yourself. Often, though, in the absence of a concise primer, you end up scouring various websites and publications, over time synthesizing a body of basic knowledge that you wished had been available as a single source.

This book is intended to serve such a purpose for North American natural gas markets. Over the years that we have managed such trading desks, we often wished that concise primers existed for new hires, simply because it would get people up to speed faster and would reduce the amount of time spent on ad hoc instruction. The material surveyed and the depth of coverage is intended for newcomers to the natural gas markets, as well as for those engaged in closely related activities who would like to understand how these markets trade. Here we are thinking in particular of investors and private equity shops who, equipped with a better understanding of the way these markets are traded, would be better positioned in their dealings with energy marketers, hedge providers and external advisors.

The book is structured in three parts, the first of which begins with a narration of key historical developments and market "color" superimposed on historical price dynamics. This is followed by a survey of essential facts of energy markets broadly, from broad topics such as global trends in production and consumption of various energy sources, to arcane but important matters such as the units in which these commodities are traded. The third chapter continues in much the same fashion, but with a deeper dive into natural gas markets.

The second part covers what most people would call market fundamentals—the key facts and trends in the way natural gas is produced, moved, stored and ultimately consumed. This part is divided into what can loosely be thought of as market drivers that affect macro price levels, supply and demand, and drivers that directly impact spreads between prices at different times and locations, in this case storage and transport.

The third and final part of this book covers trading, with a particular emphasis on the challenges arising from limitations in market liquidity. The topic of the first chapter in this part is what we refer to as price level trading, a simplistic term for trades that yield direct exposure to a change in price level, as opposed to spreads. This chapter introduces many of the primary instruments used by traders to put on risk and effect a view (in the forbidden vernacular, to "speculate") or to hedge risks in an existing portfolio. Our examples here, as well as in the following chapters, focus on the hedging of risks arising from bona fide client flow. In the second and third chapters of this final part we turn to the trading of spreads: time spreads, meaning trades which simultaneously buy and sell natural gas at two different delivery times; and locational spreads more commonly referred to as basis.

Finally, in the last chapter we discuss options trading. In full candor, we debated whether or not to include a chapter on options, a topic that could be a book in its own right. In keeping with our goal of covering what we ourselves wished our new hires would know, we chose to include this chapter. It is, however, a survey at a much higher level than the previous three chapters, focusing less on trading mechanics and more on terminology, key concepts and structures that commonly trade.

Even at a relatively modest 200 pages or so, producing such a work inevitably involves the direct support and the remarkable patience of our colleagues and families, to whom we broadly say "thank you" for putting up with us over the period of writing. Also, and in particular, we would like to thank Adviti Muni for taking a massive amount of data and draft figures, and using Tableau, producing the graphics that appear here. In addition, she proofed the draft from front to back on more than one occasion, reducing the number of typos and grammatical errors by an order of magnitude in the process.

Finally, we would like to thank Greg Stadnyk for his excellent work in the graphic design and typesetting of the book, as well as for his patience and constructive advice throughout.

Introduction

NATURAL GAS HAS been a major source of energy for the world for many decades now, with an array of applications, from highly visible heating and electricity generation, to critical industrial applications including the manufacture of fertilizers and plastics. Roughly 25% of total U.S. energy demand is met by natural gas, a figure exceeded only by crude oil and related products. Often overshadowed in public forums by renewables, dramatic changes in the technology used to produce and transport natural gas have propelled it to the forefront of fossil fuels, displacing far more carbon intensive commodities such as coal.

Natural gas is primarily methane. When methane burns it releases water, carbon dioxide and most importantly energy. Natural gas has both advantages and disadvantages in comparison to other fossil fuels. On the positive side, natural gas is much less carbon intensive per unit energy than oil or coal. Rising international concern about global warming has rendered this an increasingly important attribute. Another useful feature is that natural gas is relatively uniform in nature; whatever is produced at the wellhead is easily stripped of other gases or liquids to yield what is primarily methane. In comparison, the chemical composition of crude oils and coals can vary substantially and are much more difficult and expensive to render uniform. This relative chemical simplicity makes valuation and therefore, commerce much easier—you know exactly what you are getting. On the flip side, however, transporting natural gas is technologically challenging, at least in comparison to oil and coal which are relatively straightforward to move and store.

Natural gas requires networks of pipelines and storage facilities on land, and extremely costly shipping technology to transport globally.

The infrastructure required to support broad use of natural gas is expensive. Pipelines and storage facilities are required in addition to the obvious need to explore and develop producing fields. In the U.S., in which a deregulated market paradigm has been in play since the early 1990s, these activities requiring financing and hedging, and ultimately functional markets. In these markets spot prices are established daily at dozens of delivery locations, reflecting the cost to procure natural gas for immediate delivery. Liquid futures markets facilitate long term hedging of production and consumption. Dealers offer a variety of financing and hedging structures. Many companies and trading shops are active in the market on a daily basis.

It is the activities of these market participants and the mechanics of how risk is transferred, what trades are used, and how value is established across varying delivery tenors and locations that are the primary topics of what follows. In the first chapter, we survey the history of the markets through observable price series and metrics of trading activity, highlighting the key events along the way. In the second chapter we discuss energy markets broadly and the role of natural gas as but one of its components. Natural gas must be viewed, not as a standalone commodity, but as one that interacts with other commodities. Here we survey the global energy markets and some basic facts about energy commodities. This is followed in the third chapter by discussion of the main components of the natural gas complex, the drivers of trading activity and the various market participants.

CHAPTER 1

A Brief History of Natural Gas Prices

ALL COMMODITIES MARKETS are interesting in one way or another. Each has its own fundamental drivers, as well as idiosyncrasies in market mechanics and behavioral attributes of its participants. Every commodity meanders through its unique trajectory of random variations in supply and demand, technological innovation and market sophistication. Natural gas is no exception. Both in the U.S. and globally, natural gas markets are currently in a period of considerable upheaval. However, as we will see in a moment, this is by no means unusual. Across the past two decades there has rarely been a dull moment. Natural gas is a challenging arena in which to operate.

Modern markets in natural gas started in the 1990s. The first futures contract was launched on the NYMEX in 1990. We will talk about futures contracts in great detail later, but for now it suffices to say that commodities futures (and natural gas among them) involve delivery of a commodity over a given calendar month in the future. Futures contracts, in particular popular and highly liquid ones like the natural gas (NG) futures traded on the CME/NYMEX exchange, are useful because they yield reliable pricing information for traders and investors alike[1]. So, when the NYMEX settled (which means published an end-of-day price for) the Jan18 futures contract at $3.303 per MMBtu[2] on 7/28/2017, we know with confidence that natural gas delivered

---

[1] In fact, due to the peculiar nature of the short term "cash" or "spot" markets, natural gas futures are in many respects more reliable as price signals than various spot price indices that we will discuss later.
[2] We will discuss units in Chapter 2. A BTU is an archaic yet still commonly used unit of energy in the British system; MM is common trading notation for a million, M referring to thousands in Roman numerals.

at a particular location in Louisiana in the upcoming January was trading very near that price at the end of that particular day. We consider this price data reliable because many trades were occurring at or near this price at that time. This is useful information, especially given that we have many years of it at our disposal.

Figure 1.1 shows the trajectory of natural gas futures prices through the 1990s.

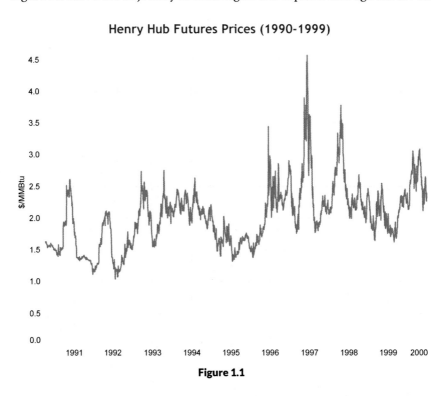

Henry Hub Futures Prices (1990-1999)

Figure 1.1

The price shown is the price in $/MMBtu of the first traded contract. We will discuss this more in Chapter 3, but for now the key fact is that futures contracts expire just before the delivery month starts, so the price series shown is just the concatenation of these distinct contract prices. The 1990s can be thought of as the primordial period for modern natural gas markets. The deployment of natural gas-fired generation en bulk, which significantly altered the way both natural gas and electricity markets interacted, only really started near the end of that decade. Prior to this its usage was mainly for home heating and various industrial processes.

The main take-away from this figure, is that price volatility was significant— at least compared to what most traders are used to in other asset classes. Between 1995 and 1997, for example, the maximum prices achieved were easily double those of the minimum, and the periods between high and low levels were relatively short. It was not that prices were just trending up or down; rather they were changing by large percentages over a matter of weeks and months. Moreover, the price "spikes" were not always in the winter, where heating demand can result in scarcity-driven premia. It was during this early period that people began to fully appreciate the risk management challenges associated with the trading of natural gas.

Figure 1.2 adds the period from 2000 to 2003 to the previous plot.

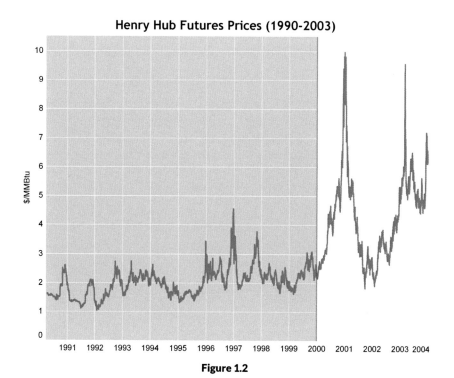

Figure 1.2

The range of price variation has now expanded dramatically. In comparison, the previous decade, which just a moment ago we deemed turbulent in its own right, now looks relatively tame. As we will see, these large swings in price can be attributed directly to changes in natural gas inventory—low inventory levels yielding the highest prices and conversely.

Partly as a consequence of this volatility, but also due to proliferation of dubious accounting practices, this period witnessed the collapse of a number of large merchant energy traders. The most well-known of these was Enron, the bankruptcy of which was followed shortly by the demise of others, among them Dynegy and Mirant. Starting in the late 1990s, these energy companies had grown from small, unremarkable physical energy asset operators into large trading operations which engaged both in aggressive speculative activities as well as dealer-oriented activities in which they acted as liquidity providers. In many respects, they served much the same function in energy markets that banks have in financial markets. The Enron bankruptcy in 2001 heralded the end of this era.

Failure of these merchants resulted in a drop in energy trading activity in all U.S. energy markets, particularly in natural gas and electricity. Vacuums like this tend to be short-lived. Propelled by cheap credit and aggressive appetites for expansion into any and all markets, numerous banks started energy marketing and trading operations, which often complemented existing energy investment banking activities. New entrants included Deutsche Bank, Credit Suisse, JPMorgan and Barclays who joined the ranks of long standing commodities traders such as Morgan Stanley and Goldman Sachs. These energy trading desks, as well as numerous hedge funds with an energy focus, were often founded and staffed by alumni of the now defunct energy merchants.

Most of these new entrants began trading near the beginning of the next epoch shown in Figure 1.3.

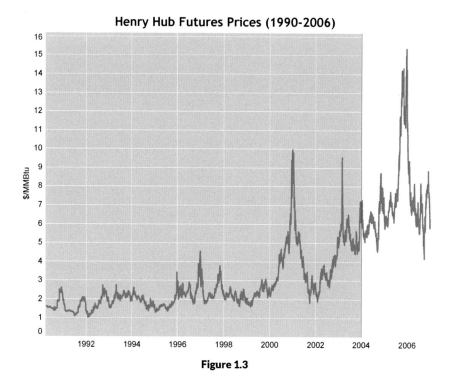

Figure 1.3

Once again, price variations meaningfully exceeded those experienced previously, driven by hurricanes Rita and Katrina which wreaked havoc in the
Gulf of Mexico in the fall of 2005. This price volatility was a wild ride for
the new trading desks. The basic thesis underpinning the bank's strategy was
that the hedging activities that are often required in tandem with lending
and investment banking were best housed under the same roof. The price
fluctuations during this period challenged this basic thesis. In addition, this
period of high energy prices resulted in the migration of some natural gas
intensive industries overseas to less expensive markets.

Things did not get any better in the following period shown in Figure 1.4
which spans the final stages of the global bull market run and the subsequent
credit crisis induced price collapse.

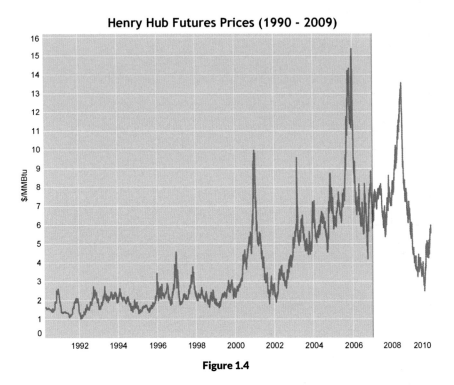

Figure 1.4

The run-up in prices prior to mid-2008 is often ascribed to unruly commodities traders whose speculative activities were no longer based on market fundamentals—whatever that statement is supposed to mean. This train of thought, which resulted in a puzzling focus on commodities as a manipulated asset class, was at best naive and at worst distracting from far more challenging issues. It is important to bear in mind that at this time the broader global economy was described by many (if not the overwhelming majority of) economists in terms of the decoupling of new economies from older and aging western ones. The thesis was that Asia's potential for growth was essentially unbounded, with the ancillary conclusion that their appetites for commodities would grow commensurately. A few prescient researchers presented contrarian views before the collapse that followed, but they were a distinct minority.

Given this broad bullish sentiment, which in hindsight was clearly flawed, a logical response was to maintain a long position in (i.e. buy) commodities. Call options on crude oil struck at $200 traded during this period—implying that some traders were willing to put money behind the view that oil prices would exceed that level in the near future. We will see later that a number of natural gas and oil producers transacted structured hedges with an embedded bullish orientation—hedges that later went terribly wrong when prices fell to under 30% of the highs. As the bubble burst and the decoupling myth was debunked, prices across all assets classes collapsed, including all energy markets.

Eventually global energy prices stabilized—with two notable exceptions: natural gas and electricity in North America. Figure 1.5 shows the last, and quite prolonged, epoch from the post-credit crisis stabilization to the present.

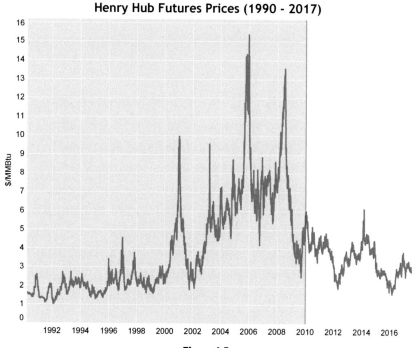

Henry Hub Futures Prices (1990 - 2017)

Figure 1.5

This period can be described as a slow grind downward driven by a huge expansion of unconventional methods of natural gas extraction, particularly fracking used in shale gas fields. Along the way there were a few significant swings in prices upward which afforded producers moments of optimism, but to date these have proven to be fleeting.

Sustained low-price regimes tend to be hard on the dealers—the banks and larger energy firms that support market liquidity and provide hedges to end users. Producers tend not to do much long-term hedging when prices are low. Locking in the value of future production at such low prices would simply serve to guarantee marginal profitability, if not outright losses. In such a situation waiting and hoping can be a better strategy than hedging. One would think, however, that by symmetry consumers, who benefit from low prices, would have the opposite reaction and hedge to lock in gains. Empirically, however, most consumers are much less inclined toward long term hedging, especially smaller end-users for whom energy consumption is a relatively minor part of their total business or household expenses.

The impact of reduced flow on the profitability of commodities trading desks, reinforced by a strong (and arguably misguided) regulatory imperative for banks to reduce their commodities footprint, resulted in many of the dealers that had entered the business but a few years earlier winding down and exiting energy trading. Another vacuum was created. This one, however, has been longer lived. A few of the traditional commodities trading houses such as Castleton and Mercuria, as well as marketing and trading desks embedded in the large energy companies such as Shell, BP and EDF, have attempted to fill some of the void. Nonetheless, it remains more challenging for end users or project developers to effect the hedges required by lenders and investors than in the prior epochs.

The ebb and flow of the natural gas markets can also be viewed from the perspective of market activity. Figure 1.6 shows the total open interest (the number of futures contracts held by market participants) from 1995 to the present.

Henry Hub Futures Total Open Interest (1995 - 2017)

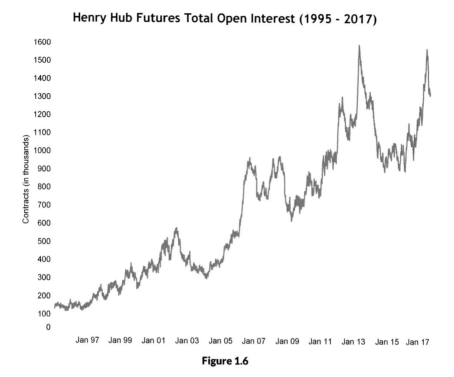

Figure 1.6

The first thing that meets the eye is that the amount of trading activity, at least by this measure, grew over ten-fold during this period. A closer look validates some of the points made earlier. First, the drop in open interest in 2003 coincided roughly with the demise of the energy merchants. We are not doing the sequential addition of data to figures as we did for prices above, so it is important to note that this was nearly a 50% fall in open interest. This was a huge drop in trading activity. The fluctuations in the 2007-2008 period, while not quite so severe, were large nonetheless, falling roughly a third.

Things became a bit more complex after the credit crisis. Futures contracts are one among several commonly traded instruments. An important feature of futures is that they are exchange traded, as opposed to over-the-counter (OTC) trades which are bilateral transactions between two counterparties and which are not traded on exchanges. The open interest time series shown above, therefore, measures only a subset of all natural gas trades. The growth in market activity witnessed in the years since the credit crisis was in large part due to the regulatory imperative to use futures contracts in lieu of OTC trades. Many large trading shops worked together to novate their OTC contracts to futures exchanges. This explains, at least in part, the overall trend in open interest.

The large fluctuations in price in this period were usually the result of perceived trends and changing market views. When prices rose, producers reengaged their longer-term hedging programs. In addition, changes in the fundamental landscape drove trading activity. After a relatively mild winter in early 2016 and a resulting price drop, open interest began to increase as some market participants developed a bullish view based on the notion that domestic production was likely to fall and that exports would increase. This view persisted through roughly the first half of 2017 until enthusiasm for this trade diminished due to continued price stagnation.

The value of any commodity depends both upon when you have it and where you have it. Time and location matter—a theme that will appear throughout what follows. Benchmark futures prices like the NG contract that we have been discussing so far tell us a lot about the time component of price dynamics, but provide little if any useful information about the locational component. Natural gas markets in the U.S. have many dozens of distinct pricing points, or hubs. Prices where natural gas is produced are systematically lower than in places where consumption is high—for example, metropolitan areas in cold regions where heating demand can overwhelm available supply. A great deal of trading activity relates to locational price spreads. A physical natural gas trading operation will typically have an order of magnitude more staff involved in locational trading (what we call basis trading) than those focusing on the benchmark futures.

Basis markets present their own challenges, especially in recent times. Figure 1.7 shows the average monthly spread between spot prices at a location near New York City[3] where there is high winter heating demand and Henry Hub, Louisiana over the past decade.

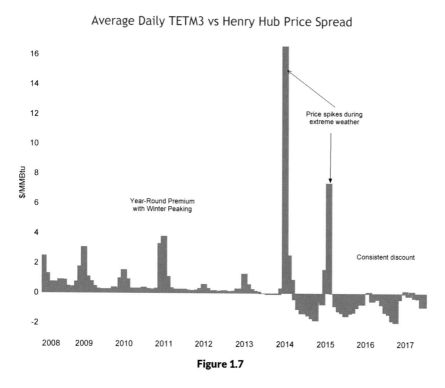

Figure 1.7

For years, a premium was the norm. If you were on a trading desk at any time in the 2000s, you would simply know and take for granted that the northeastern hubs were always premium to locations in the Gulf Coast, and in winter months massively so. In recent years, however, the situation has been completely upended. Increased shale gas production has altered locational price dynamics. This formerly premium location and many others are now realizing at a meaningful discount for all but the coldest time periods, and in recent winters the price spread has been essentially zero. Some basis traders have simply quit in disgust; their knowledge and training rendered obsolete in the new environment. Naturally their seats are filled by more optimistic individuals.

---

3 TETM3, short for the TETCO M3 delivery zone, will be appear repeatedly in the following chapters.

Natural gas markets are fundamentally non-stationary. At no point over the past 15 years should anyone have believed that things had stabilized and become more predictable, and the changes continue unabated. A number of factors are in play which are likely to dampen the effects of shale production, pulling the markets back toward what might be viewed as a more reasonable state. Gas-fired electricity generation is displacing coal plants. Industrial users have been repatriating activities such as fertilizer and plastics production. Exports to Mexico have been increasing. Liquefied natural gas (LNG) export facilities, some originally constructed with an intention to import into high priced U.S. markets and subsequently converted for export, are sprouting up as regulatory impediments to export are reduced. Pipeline expansions are increasing transport capacity from shale producing regions.

All of these developments are sensible market responses to the price environment as it currently stands. Will these equilibrating forces be overdone, overshooting and pushing markets too high? Will other unanticipated developments jar the markets out of local equilibria? As of the time of writing, large swathes of the U.S. had just experienced a polar vortex redux, with record setting cold temperatures, coupled with extremely high demand and prices, the consequences of which are still playing out. If Figure 1.5 communicates anything, it is that natural gas will likely remain an interesting and challenging arena. The remaining chapters are intended to provide a set of essential information for anyone involved in trading, structuring or origination in natural gas.

CHAPTER 2

The Global Energy Landscape

GLOBAL ENERGY CONSUMPTION is dominated by fossil fuels. Crude oil, and the associated palette of refined products such as gasoline and heating oil, is the largest market. This is followed closely in size by coal and natural gas. Each of these commodities are broadly traded, with crude oil and coal truly global markets with significant transport occurring between regions. Each of these has its own distinct uses. Most cars still burn gasoline. The manufacture of plastics and fertilizers relies heavily on natural gas. Certain types of coal are required for steel production. However, some aspects of our energy usage are fungible in the sense that more than one of these energy sources can be used to accomplish the same thing. Electricity generation and home heating are two examples. As a result of such substitutability, global energy markets are inextricably intertwined.

The interaction of energy markets can sometimes be seen in prices. One relationship that was commonly discussed on trading desks for many years was the joint behavior of crude oil and natural gas shown in Figure 2.1 from 2000 to 2008. Here we are showing two U.S. benchmark energy prices: WTI for oil and NG for natural gas. WTI is a specific type of crude oil delivered in Oklahoma and NG refers to natural gas delivered in Louisiana[4]. We have normalized each price series by its average over this period to facilitate comparison, so that these are unit-free representations of the historical prices.

---

4 The time series are the rolling calendar strips, which will define this precisely later; for the moment think of this as the cost of the commodity averaged over the upcoming year.

Normalized Crude Oil and Natural Gas Prices

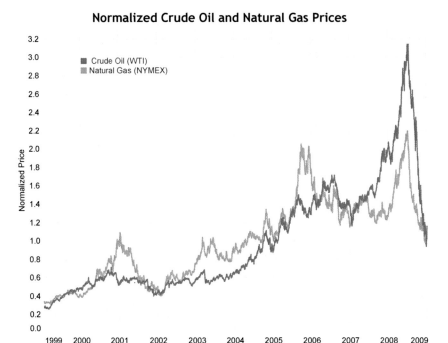

Figure 2.1

At first glance these two series seem to have something to do with each other, and this apparent relationship was commonly discussed on energy trading desks for most of the time period shown here. The existence of a relationship is plausible—in addition to some substitutability, global macroeconomic drivers are relevant to each, since both oil (and the refined products derived from it) and natural gas are used heavily in industrial processes. Whether or not a defensible statistical relationship between these prices actually existed, the fact that trading desks were interested in it, and traded accordingly, at least somewhat coupled these markets.

Another example appears in Figure 2.2. Here we show two additional benchmark price series: PJM Peak , which is a U.S. electricity price, and Newcastle coal , an Australian coal index commonly referenced in Asian markets[5].

---

5   We chose Newcastle as it supports a futures market that provides useful price transparency. A similar benchmark in the U.S. which referenced Central Appalachian coal prices was recently discontinued as a futures contract.

Normalized Energy Benchmark Prices

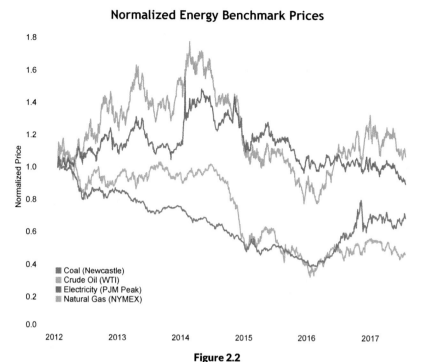

Figure 2.2

In this figure, we have normalized each price series by its value at the beginning of 2012. Although all energy prices fell consistently from 2014 to 2016, any notion of a useful relationship between oil and natural gas seems far less compelling than it did in the previous figure. During this period shale production of both crude oil and natural gas was driving everything down, but these markets were responding in different ways. Another observation is the close coupling between natural gas and electricity prices, a relationship originating in the large-scale deployment of natural gas-fired generation in the U.S. The fluctuations of relative value between electricity and natural gas was due in part to interactions between different types of generation sourcing different fuels.

The point of such examples is that before embarking on a discussion of (let alone trading in) a particular market such as natural gas, it is useful to know something about the other related markets.

Global Energy Usage

Figure 2.3 shows total global energy consumption by source in common units of metric ton oil equivalent (mtoe) (BP)

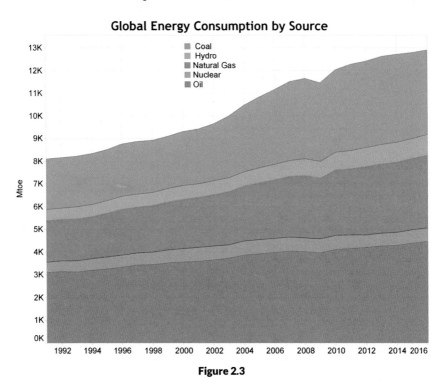

Figure 2.3

The overall trend has been a relentless increase in total energy usage. The aftermath of the credit crisis was the only period where growth was significantly negative. It is perhaps surprising that this somewhat small departure (at least optically) from the overall trend resulted in the roughly 70% drop in prices that we saw in Figure 1.4.

A natural question is just how relevant energy consumption is in the broader economy. In 2016 annual global consumption was approaching 13 billion mtoe, which equates to the energy content of approximately 95 billion barrels of crude oil. Taking a reference crude oil price of say $50 per barrel, this amounts to a notional value of almost 5 trillion USD. For comparison global GDP in 2016 was approximately 75 trillion USD. This is a "back-of-the-envelope" calculation, since the cost of energy varies by source. It is clear, however, that energy usage is a meaningful component of global economic activity.

Units and Orders of Magnitude

We have just encountered one obstacle to interpreting energy supply and demand statistics, namely the variety of units used. A few basic conversions and rules of thumb are useful.

Most trading in crude oil and refined products references either barrels, gallons or metric tons to define notional quantities. These are volumetric and weight units, as opposed to energy units such as MMBtus (an MMBtu is one million British Thermal Units) or gigaJoules (gJs) One barrel of crude oil is equivalent to:

- 42 gallons
- Approximately 5.4 MMBtu
- .1364 metric tons

Natural gas trading references both volumetric units (cubic feet or cubic meters) and energy units (MMBtus, also referred to as dekatherms, or gigaJoules. One MMBtu is equivalent to:

- Approximately 1000 cubic feet (cf) of natural gas
- 1.05 gJ
- .025 metric tons of crude oil

Many electricity and natural gas markets are closely coupled due to the increasing deployment of combined cycle generation in many parts of the world. Electricity is always measured in units of megawatt-hours (MWhs) or kilowatt-hours (kWhs). An efficient combined cycle generator running at full output requires just under 7 MMBtus of natural gas to produce one MWh of electricity, which is enough to power approximately 1000 U.S. households for one hour[6].

Global Production and Consumption Patterns

The relative contributions of the various energy sources to global consumption evolves over time, driven both by relative price, technological innovations and regulation. Figure 2.4 shows the state-of-affairs in 2016 using the same categories as the previous figure.

2016 Global Energy Consumption by Source

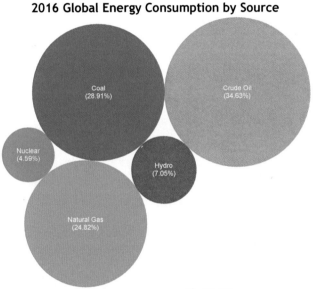

Figure 2.4

The three primary fossil fuels comprise close to 90% of all energy consumed globally, although this is changing. From 2014 to 2016 there was a 4% decline in coal consumption in absolute terms. Most of this drop was replaced by natural gas, although the footprint of renewable energy sources continues to grow. Non-hydro renewables, a category that includes wind, solar and geothermal,

---

6 Household usage varies dramatically by location. Many U.S. households consume far more than this conversion implies, so it should be viewed as a convenient "rule-of-thumb" for quick conversion.

still comprise a rather paltry 3.1% of global usage in 2016 (BP). That said, in comparison to 2.8% in 2015, one can argue that this was in fact an impressive year-on-year increase of over 10%. If this growth rate continues the profile of global energy usage will be dramatically different in the future.

Changes in the relative contributions of our energy sources may be relatively slow, but the same cannot be said about geographic distribution. Figure 2.5 shows consumption by region for the years 2000 and 2016 (BP).

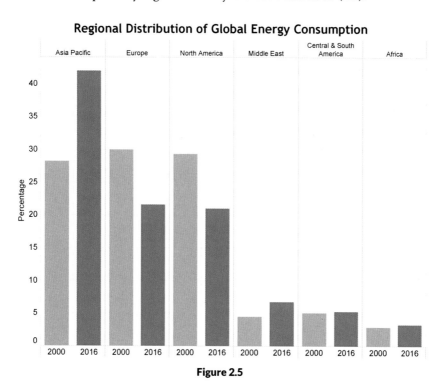

Figure 2.5

For most of the 20th century, consumption was substantially concentrated in North America and Europe. However, by 2003 the Asia Pacific region had assumed the lead, due in large part to the migration of industrial activity from western countries to China. By region it is now, by far, the largest energy consumer.

As the largest energy source and the most actively traded energy commodity, the headline facts about crude oil are well known. Most consumption occurs in North America, Europe and Asia. Figure 2.6 shows consumption in 2000 and 2016 (BP).

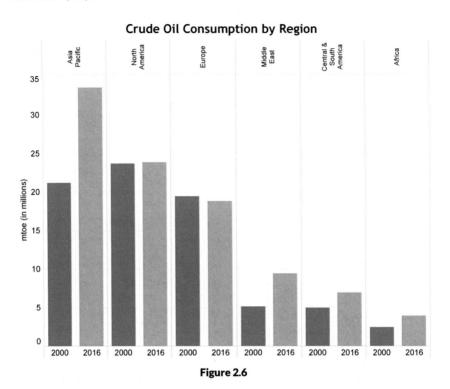

Figure 2.6

Production in these years is shown in Figure 2.7.

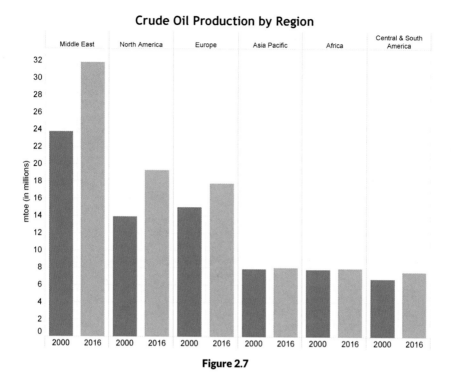

Figure 2.7

There has been a great deal of press related to increased production in North America, but it is interesting that the Middle East has quietly witnessed a similar increase. Moreover, the big-ticket item remains the increase in consumption in Asia.

Figure 2.8 emphasizes this last point, showing net oil consumption by region.

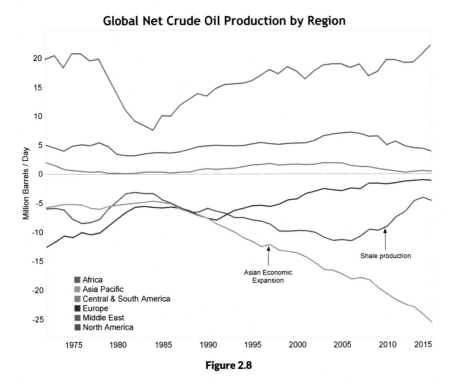

Figure 2.8

While North America had indeed sunk to a meaningful deficit in the 2000s, in recent years its net production has returned to levels typical of the 70s and 80s. It is the change in Asian consumption that truly stands out.

These regional imbalances are resolved via transportation of large amounts of crude oil around the globe, primarily by tanker. This makes crude oil an inherently global commodity. Pricing relationships can be complex due to the variety of grades of crude, shipping costs and trade restrictions, but oil is, to a large degree, global and fungible. If price differentials between two grades of crude delivered at two different locations depart too far from "normal", shipping and refining technology will usually force an equilibration.

Natural gas markets, in contrast, are much less global in nature. It is simply harder to ship substances that are gases, which must be either compressed or liquefied before loading onto tankers, than fuels which are solids or liquid at standard temperatures and pressures. For many years there was minimal intercontinental commerce in natural gas. Technology has evolved, however, and an expanding fleet of liquid natural gas (LNG) tankers and supporting infrastructure is reducing the cost of overseas transport. In conjunction with rapidly growing production in the U.S., the prevailing view is that natural gas will ultimately evolve into a commodity that is globally traded much as crude oil is now.

Statistics for natural gas usage are typically quoted in billion cubic feet (bcf) per day. As of 2016 global consumption stood at roughly 350 bcf/day, which amounts to 70% of crude oil usage in energy content. The regional distribution of production is shown in Figure 2.9 for the same two reference years of 2000 and 2016 (BP).

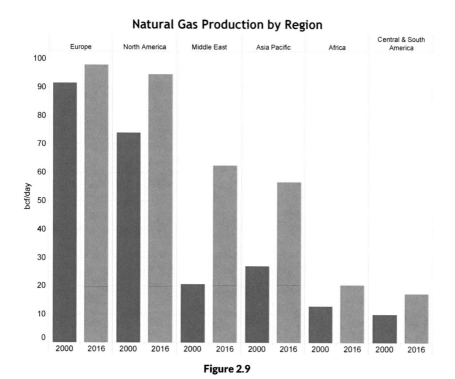

Figure 2.9

The largest increases were seen in the Middle East and Asia, with North America registering a slightly smaller, but still significant 25% increase.

Changes in consumption patterns are actually quite similar, as seen in Figure 2.10 (BP).

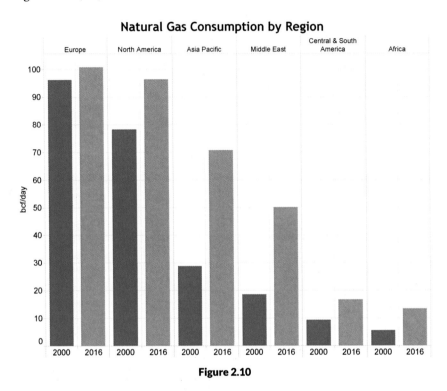

Figure 2.10

From the perspective of net production however, circumstances have changed dramatically.

Figure 2.11 shows the evolution of net production by region.

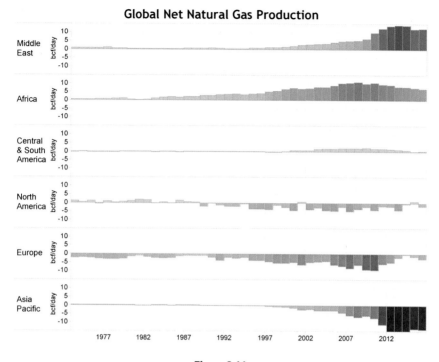

Figure 2.11

The growing Middle East surplus is due in part to expansion of infrastructure supporting liquefied natural gas (LNG) transport. This has resulted in supply that in earlier times had been viewed as an essentially worthless by-product of oil production, and which would have simply been flared at the wellhead[7].

In the Asia/Pacific region, although we saw that rates of both production and consumption had grown substantially, the deficit continues to expand. Less dramatic, but certainly more surprising, is the rise in North American production since 2005 due to shale gas and the reversal of the prior trend toward ever increasing deficits as Gulf production waned.

---

7   Flaring refers to burning natural gas rather than simply emitting it. While seemingly wasteful, flaring is far better from an environmental perspective than releasing methane, which is both toxic and of substantially higher greenhouse impact.

Natural Gas Flows

The two primary methods for transporting natural gas are by pipeline or as LNG[8]. Figure 2.12 shows the quantity of natural gas flow volumes by pipeline and by LNG shipping, as well as net import volumes (BP). The last column shows the greater of imports and exports as a percentage of total consumption. We have chosen this as a measure of how coupled a particular market is to other markets, as opposed to say net flows which could be minimal even with large imports and exports.

(Billion Cubic Feet(BCF) per day)

Flow by Pipeline

Region	Imports	Exports	Net	Consumption	Percentage
Asia Pacific	3.30	0.00	3.30	69.71	4.74
Europe & Eurasia	4.37	3.97	0.40	99.38	4.40
Middle East & Africa	0.67	4.37	0.00	62.80	6.97
North America	0.00	0.00	0.00	93.40	0.00
South & Central America	0.00	0.00	0.00	16.59	0.00

Flow by LNG

Region	Imports	Exports	Net	Consumption	Percentage
Asia Pacific	11.08	0.22	10.86	69.71	15.90
Europe & Eurasia	5.01	1.92	3.09	99.38	5.04
Middle East & Africa	0.58	14.47	0.00	62.80	23.05
North America	0.43	0.35	0.00	93.40	0.46
South & Central America	0.77	1.24	0.00	16.59	7.46

Figure 2.12

There are several important points to be gleaned from this data. First interregional pipeline flows are minimal. Within the Americas and Europe pipelines are the dominant mechanism for balancing locational variations in supply and demand. However, pipelines do essentially nothing to couple distinct geographic regions—at least as we have chosen to define them here. LNG is a different matter, significantly coupling Asia (16% LNG ratio) and the Middle East (23% LNG ratio). To date both North America and South & Central America remain functionally decoupled from other markets, although this is almost certainly going to change in the upcoming years with

---

8   There are other methods such as compressed natural gas (CNG), but at present these play a significantly smaller role.

continuing development of export facilities and favorable regulatory developments in the United States.

A final comment on the results discussed above. These regions are big, and there is a lot going on within each region that is simply not visible in the results presented. Europe & Eurasia includes countries such as Germany, Netherlands and Ukraine, which are heavily dependent on exports from Russia. In the greater Asia Pacific region, Australia, and to a lesser extent Malaysia and Indonesia, export large quantities of natural gas to China and Japan. Intra-regional commerce in natural gas is an expansive and complex topic in its own right.

Relevance of Electricity Markets

Electricity is, in a sense, at the top of the food chain among energy commodities—all natural energy resources are used to some extent to produce it. Moreover, almost everyone is a direct consumer of electricity—few things petrify a society quite like the fear of a prolonged and expansive blackout.

To put the magnitude of electricity consumption in perspective, just under 25,000 terawatt hours of electricity were generated globally in 2016. If we viewed this in units of mtoe, this would imply that electricity generation accounts for roughly 16% of global energy usage. However, roughly two thirds of this electricity was produced by the combustion of fossil fuels (IEA, 2016). Given that even the most efficient fossil fuel generation has conversion efficiencies of the order of 50%, electricity actually counts for closer to 25% of total energy consumption.

The general global trends and regional statistics of electricity generation mirror global energy trends shown earlier. The major producers (and consumers, since intra-regional transmission is minimal) are North America, Europe & Eurasia and the Asia Pacific, with Asia Pacific dominating since

2003 (BP). There was also a drop in electricity generation in 2009, similar to what occurred in global energy usage. This is noteworthy as up to that point electricity consumption had increased without interruption since the early part of the 20th century.

In parts of North America, supply increases resulting from shale gas and the contemporaneous expansion of gas-fired generation capacity have largely decoupled natural gas and electricity from global energy markets. We saw evidence of this earlier in Figure 2.2 where the prices of U.S. benchmarks for both electricity and natural gas are visibly coupled with each other, but have little apparent relationship to international energy benchmarks.

Figure 2.13 shows historical electricity generation by year as estimated by the EIA for different categories of generation.

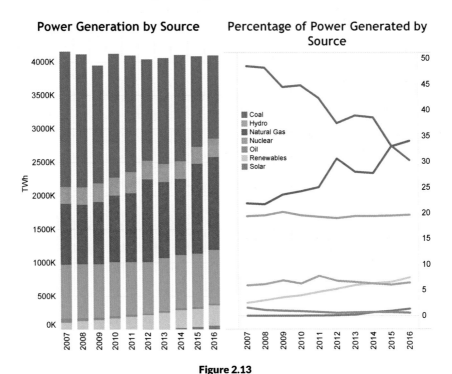

Figure 2.13

Several features stand out. First, the drop in consumption in 2009 at the apex of the credit crisis is clearly visible. Second, natural gas has definitively displaced coal as the primary energy source for electricity generation. The drop in coal usage has been precipitous, falling from just under 50% to roughly 30% in a single decade. The environmental benefits from this displacement are substantial, with comparatively lower emissions of greenhouse gases and other sundry unpleasantries such as sulfur dioxide and mercury emissions. However, environmental concerns were not the primary driving force behind this change. It was (and remains) a matter of price. Falling natural gas prices and improvements in gas-fired generation technology made the economic benefits of a switch from coal to natural gas compelling.

Natural gas plays such an important role in the price dynamics of electricity that one cannot reasonably expect to trade electricity without also trading natural gas. The vast majority of electricity trading desks also trade natural gas to some extent. Those whose activities involve the outright purchase or sale of electricity (as opposed to the trading of arcane spreads in the electricity markets) typically rely heavily on natural gas markets to hedge their positions.

CHAPTER 3

Natural Gas Markets

COMMODITIES MARKETS SERVE two basic purposes. The first is to balance supply and demand on short time horizons, whether this be the next hour in electricity markets, the next few days in natural gas or even the upcoming weeks or months for oil and coal. The second is to provide a venue for trading instruments which can be used to ensure price stability over longer time horizons—so called hedging activities. In this chapter we will survey natural gas markets from the perspective of these activities, including the types of market participants and the activities and organization of trading desks.

Spot Price Risk

Trading activity in which commodities are bought and sold for (near) immediate delivery is referred to as "spot trading" or "cash trading". An example of cash trading is when a utility needs to procure natural gas for its customers as forecasted for tomorrow. The utility must find someone who has natural gas to sell and negotiate a price for delivery of the required quantity.

Figure 3.1 shows the daily price (the spot price) for natural gas delivered at TETCO M3, a commonly traded delivery location in the northeastern U.S. which we will refer to as TETM3 going forward.

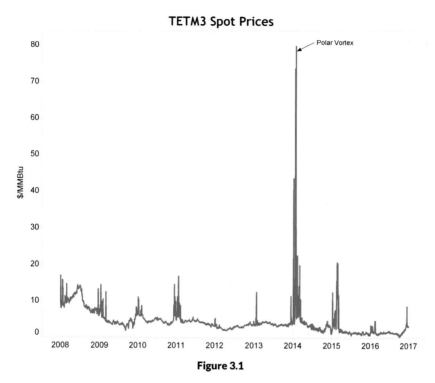

Figure 3.1

This price is an index compiled by Bloomberg and should be thought of as representative of the price at which natural gas transacted for each delivery day. It is in essence a volumetric average of the relevant trading prices. Details aside, the salient feature is the extreme variation in prices that can occur, over both long and short time scales. If you need to procure natural gas on a daily basis and your strategy is to buy it in the spot market, then you will directly experience the effects of these price fluctuations. This is spot price risk.

The Commodities Lifecycle and Price Fluctuations

A commodity is something that is extracted or grown, transported, transformed, and ultimately consumed. The lifecycle of an energy commodity usually resembles the illustration in Figure 3.2.

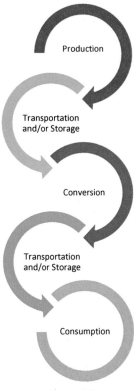

Figure 3.2

The first stage is production. This is usually followed by transport, since consumers tend not to live close to centers of production, whether mines or wells. In most cases the commodity must be transformed into something that can be used. Examples include the refining of crude oil and the stripping of impurities from natural gas. Finally, the timing of consumer demand is often not coincident with when the commodity is produced—in the U.S. natural gas is produced at a relatively uniform rate throughout each year, while consumption is heavily concentrated in the winter months due to heating demand. Storage facilities effectively transport the commodity through time, thereby resolving this temporal mismatch. The final stage is consumption—the commodity is burned to release energy or used as inputs for various industrial processes.

The details of each of these activities varies by commodity. It is the nature of each stage that determines price dynamics. For natural gas the life cycle looks as follows:

- Production: This stage typically involves natural gas wells located both on land (on-shore) and in the oceans (off-shore).
- Transport: Most transport occurs via pipelines from the wellhead to local processing and storage, and ultimately to end users. Increasingly, liquefied natural gas (LNG) transport, in which natural gas is cooled to liquid form, transported in specialized vessels, and regasified at the destination is being used for international shipping.
- Storage: Storage usually involves modified geological structures designed to hold natural gas with minimal loss. As we will see later, the volumes are large and man-made structures alone do not suffice[9].

---

9   Storing natural gas in LNG form is expensive due to the energy needed to maintain the required low temperatures and is not typically used for anything other than very short-term storage.

- Consumption: Demand for natural gas arises primarily from:
    - Residential and commercial end-users, particularly for heating.
    - Industrial consumers for manufacturing, petrochemical and fertilizer production.
    - Electricity generation.

All stages in this lifecycle are susceptible to sudden and unpredictable change. Hurricanes can force the shutdown of large swathes of production. Equipment failures can impact pipelines and the availability of storage, particularly on extremely cold winter days when natural gas is needed most. Finally, demand can change by several multiples over the course of a few days as temperatures fluctuate. Rapid swings in demand and infrastructure performance cause the price volatility shown in Figure 3.1.

In the absence of anything other than short term trading, businesses would immediately feel the impact of spot price risk, and at the wrong time the effects could be disastrous. Paying $80/MMBtu to obtain gas for your retail customers when you thought you were going to pay $8 is a big deal, thwarting your efforts to plan for enough funds and operational capital, and agitating your investors who may be less than forgiving in the face of large and sudden losses. This is what motivates the second type of trading—hedging activities which are designed to reduce price risk to tolerable levels.

Risk Transfer and Market Participants

Markets support the transfer of price risk between producers and consumers. Market participants are often grouped into distinct categories based upon the nature of their activities and risk profiles. First, there are those on both ends of the spectrum—the producers and consumers of the commodity, both of whom have price risk as an inherent part of their businesses. The ultimately offsetting risks of the producers and consumers are often matched via intermediaries. These are dealers and hedge funds which are ready and willing to hold (or "inventory") price exposures for periods of time before finding offsetting positions, provided they think they will make money in the process. A third category consists of market facilitators which include commodities exchanges and various equity-like vehicles, particularly commonly traded index and ETF products. Finally, the activities of market participants are overseen by regulators tasked with maintaining fair and orderly markets. We will survey these in order.

- Natural Longs and Shorts

Markets exist because of the "naturals"—those with one-way price exposures arising from their businesses. Producers are the natural longs and consumers are the natural shorts[10]. In absence of any hedging activity, the former benefit when prices go up and the latter when prices go down. Although it is tempting to assume a symmetry in the risks and hedging activities of the longs and shorts, the two groups have very different risk profiles and hedging protocols.

Production involves exploration, the location of potential natural gas reservoirs, and development, in which producing wells are drilled and natural gas is gathered and delivered to the pipeline system. Production is a capital-intensive affair requiring investments in land and in equipment. These activities are funded by both shareholders and lenders, and the investment time horizons are usually of the order of years or even decades. In the absence of hedging these investments are exposed to price risk over considerable periods of time.

Consumers are a much more varied group, and their time horizons for risk management are typically much shorter than for producers. Examples of the different types of consumers are:

- Utilities: These are regulated companies that deliver natural gas and

---

10 The term "long" refers to owning something and hence benefiting from price increases. Conversely, the term "short" refers to having an obligation to obtain something, therefore benefiting from decreasing prices.

electricity to their customers, and as such are natural shorts. Many utilities also use natural gas to generate electricity. The price that utilities can charge their customers requires regulatory approval and depends upon prevailing commodity prices, as well as operating and capital costs.

- Local Distribution Companies (LDCs): LDCs are regulated entities which supply natural gas to their customers. LDCs buy and take delivery of natural gas at the meter of an interstate or intrastate pipeline and deliver the gas to end-users. On one hand LDCs can be viewed as pipeline operators without a net natural position. However, they often have an associated customer base that renders them naturally short.

- Independent Power Producers (IPPs): As unregulated companies which own and operate merchant power plants, IPPs produce electricity and sell it directly in the wholesale electricity markets. Those that own and operate natural gas-fired generation need to buy natural gas on a daily basis in order to run their units and are, therefore, natural shorts (from an electricity perspective they are natural longs).

- Energy Retailers: In some parts of the U.S., competitive retail markets exist for both natural gas and for electricity. Retail companies market and advertise their energy service programs to potential customers, ranging from large companies to individual households. Retailers have an obligation to procure the commodity for delivery as required by their customers, and as such are natural shorts.

- Industrial Consumers: Substantial volumes of natural gas are used in large-scale manufacturing and petrochemicals activities. Such industrial consumers usually purchase natural gas from utilities, energy merchants or retailers. Some companies, for example US Steel and Dow Chemical, are large enough to have their own trading desks in-house to manage price exposure and to procure the required natural gas directly from the wholesale markets.

- Hedging and Risk Intermediaries

Consumers and producers have largely offsetting risks. One way to hedge price is via a direct transaction between the two: a sale of the commodity by a natural long to a natural short. Such a transaction takes the form of a bilateral contract between the two parties resulting in delivery of defined volumes of natural gas at a defined price over some future time period, thereby directly hedging the price risk of both.

While not uncommon, this is far from the complete story of typical hedging activities. As mentioned, producers tend to worry about their price exposure over longer time horizons than do natural shorts. The lenders and shareholders of producers care a great deal about the stability of cash flows over the duration of loans and investment horizons. In contrast, utilities and retailers rarely have meaningful price exposures beyond a year or two, and their hedging activities are comparatively shorter in tenor. Matching a retailer to a producer in a bilateral trade can, therefore, be difficult.

This disparity in planning horizons limits the viability of direct hedging and requires someone to step in and match the risks of longs and shorts. This is the role of intermediaries—entities which are not naturally long or short, but which buy from the former and sell to the latter, often holding residual risk positions for extended periods of time. There are a variety of such intermediaries:

- Dealers: The term dealer typically refers to large and well-capitalized trading operations that are often part of a larger enterprises—banks or energy companies, such as Morgan Stanley, J Aron, Shell, BP and EDF.
- Commodities Trading Shops: These are companies, often private and unrated, which are involved in the physical commodities markets. They make money by, for example, purchasing natural gas in one market and transporting it to another market for a profit. They also market physical natural gas directly to end users, utilizing their assets and overall energy market prowess to maximize returns on capital. Their activities can involve acquisition of storage and transport as a part of their overall trading and marketing strategy. Examples of these types of firms are Mercuria, Vitol, Trafigura, Castleton, Glencore, and Freepoint.

- Hedge funds: These are partnerships of investors which engage in speculative trading, often using proprietary strategies. Hedge funds serve a purpose in risk intermediation as they can, if the price is right, absorb and hold significant risk positions.

- Market Facilitators

Consumers, producers, dealers and hedge funds rely heavily upon a third (and quite varied) category of market participants and investment vehicles which we will collectively refer to as market facilitators—entities whose primary mission is to make trading more efficient.

The first among these are the commodities exchanges, which match buyers and sellers, while largely insulating markets participants from credit risk. Exchanges started as "open outcry" markets, referred to as pits, in which members would match buyers and sellers by direct voice communication (one might even say yelling). These have been largely replaced with electronic trading platforms, in which traders can monitor current market prices on a screen and execute transactions with the click of a mouse (or using APIs for algorithmic execution). Exchanges mitigate credit risk through their clearing and margining protocols. We will discuss the issue of credit risk and clearing more later, but the upshot is that if you trade on an exchange your counterparty is the exchange itself, which in theory has enough capital available to render default an event of extremely low probability. The two major exchanges on which natural gas trades are the CME (owner of NYMEX) and the Intercontinental Exchange or ICE, which operates the premier over-the-counter electronic platform for natural gas.

Brokers are another important class of facilitators. The traditional broker matches buyers and sellers by maintaining lines of communication between potential buyers and sellers. Often this is done simply by phone and IM chats with those known to be involved in the market. Brokers get paid a transaction fee on executed trades.

Finally, a third category warrants mention. Exchange traded funds (ETFs) and index funds are financial instruments that trade like equities, which have price exposures customized in some way. There are a number of commodities funds which embed energy price exposures. The US Natural Gas Fund (UNG) is an ETF designed to yield returns that track those of natural gas futures prices. Commodity Index Funds are funds that are comprised of an index that follow a specific set of commodities with specified weights for each commodity and, like ETFs, can be traded in the broader market. Natural gas is included in most indices that have an embedded energy component. Examples of commodity indices are Goldman Sachs Commodity Index (GSCI), Bloomberg Commodity Index (BCOM), and Merrill Lynch Commodity Index eXtra (MLCX).

- Regulators

There are two general categories of regulation that impacts natural gas traders. The first are the regulations underpinning the very existence and form of competitive natural gas markets. The second are part of larger regulatory rubric designed to ensure market integrity and to discourage and penalize fraudulent trading practices.

In the primordial stages of the natural gas markets early last century, the train of thought was that the large amounts of capital needed to build the required infrastructure necessitated a regulated rate of return. This yielded the vertically integrated utility model in which a single company handles all aspects of natural gas services, with returns on capital set by local utility commissions. Prevailing economic paradigms have shifted over the years, and as the industry matured some parts of the natural gas supply chain were migrated to competitive markets. This occurred through several waves of deregulations orders, with the primary impetus provided by FERC Order 636, which effectively ended the natural pipeline monopolies. Pipeline companies were forced to separate their merchant commodities operations from transport and storage operations, and to provide open and fair access to pipeline capacity to all market participants.

Natural gas markets in the U.S. are now largely deregulated, with the exception being the pipeline and local distribution companies (LDCs), which remain heavily regulated. In short, the wholesale marketplace, in which participants of all sorts buy, sell and transport natural gas, is for all intents and purposes deregulated.

The regulators involved in natural gas markets include state regulators (for intrastate pipeline transactions) and public utility commissions. At a national level, the Federal Energy Regulatory Commission (FERC) is the regulator overseeing interstate activities in natural gas. The FERC is an independent federal agency that regulates natural gas, oil and electricity. For natural gas specifically, the FERC regulates interstate pipelines, storage and LNG facilities connected to such. FERC also establishes rates of service, referred to as tariffs, which control the costs charged for pipeline transport and storage thereby ensuring fair and equitable access to all market participants.

Increasingly the FERC has assumed a larger role in the second type of activity related to regulation and monitoring of trading activities, with a focus on market manipulation. The other regulator with a large footprint in this type of regulation is the Commodity Futures Trading Commission (CFTC). The CFTC was created by Congress with a mandate to regulate commodity futures and option markets in the United States. The CFTC's mission is to protect consumers and the public in general from fraudulent market manipulation.

The regulatory landscape continues to evolve, due in part to echoes from the credit crisis as well as continuing natural evolution of the markets. In spite of the changes, the basic mechanisms for trading natural gas, to which we turn next, have remained largely the same over the past two decades.

Forward Markets and Hedging

How do natural longs and shorts hedge price risk? The subsequent chapters address this question in some detail, but it is useful at this stage to have at least a conceptual understanding of what is involved. The key concept is that of a forward trade.

Forward trades are the fulcrum for trading and hedging in commodities markets. In a forward transaction two counterparties agree "now" to exchange some amount of a commodity for a fixed price at a specified time in the future and at a specified location. For example, suppose that a producer of natural gas contracted with a buyer on 30Jun2017 to sell 10,000 MMBtus per day delivered at Henry Hub, LA in the month of January 2018 at a price of $3.35/MMBtu. This is called a "forward" trade because the price is agreed upon at the time of the trade for a delivery in the future[11]. Assuming that no other trades are executed between the two counterparties, when January 2018 rolls around the seller will deliver the agreed upon volumes each day during the month and the buyer will pay the seller $3.35/MMBtu.

A forward transaction, which is closely related to futures trades on the commodities exchanges (the distinction will be discussed more in Chapter 6), involves defining the quantity of natural gas, its specifications[12], when it will be delivered, and equally importantly where it will be delivered. For delivery times and locations where demand is expected to be high, such as the Northeastern markets in the winter, forward prices will tend to be higher than for times and places where production is high and demand is low.

The importance of the concept of forward pricing cannot be over-stated. At any given moment the forward curve, which is the collection of forward prices

---

11 Technically most trades, even spot purchases for delivery tomorrow, involve a price that is agreed upon prior to delivery; after all, tomorrow is in the future. So, in a sense all trades are forward trades. It is common practice to refer to forward prices as prices pertaining to future delivery periods other than tomorrow, or whatever the spot delivery conventions are for a commodity.

12 For natural gas this is relatively simple, restricting the amount of water and other undesirable components. For crude oil, in contrast, specification is a major undertaking given the vast array of very different crude oil streams produced globally.

for all future delivery months, defines the prices at which the commodity can be bought or sold now for future delivery. If you expect to produce a certain amount of natural gas in the future, the prevailing forward curve defines the market value of that production. Figure 3.3 shows two forward curves for Henry Hub: one corresponding to 01Jul2010 and the other to 01Jul2015. Each point represents the price at the end of the trading day for each future month— the Jan17 delivery month is highlighted.

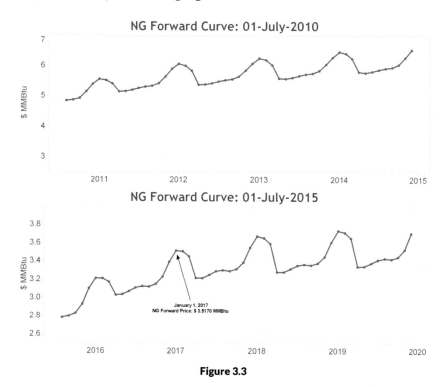

Figure 3.3

Both forward curves show higher prices in the winter than the summer— this is due to the sensible expectation of traders that prices will be higher in the winter due to heating demand. Note, however, that the second curve is both at much lower price levels and has much less seasonality (a lower spread between winter and summer prices). It is also clearly upward sloping. This particular change in forward prices, as we will see later, was a direct result of a glut of natural gas arising from the high levels of shale gas production.

Commodities exchanges and brokers in North American natural gas markets monitor and support forward trading in dozens of different delivery locations. The behavior of forward prices and the mechanics of trading will be a common thread through the subsequent chapters. The key points to keep in mind are:

- Forward prices almost always reference calendar delivery months, with a single forward curve comprised of a set of individual monthly prices.
- A hedger wishing to buy or sell a commodity across a set of future delivery months can do so at or near the prevailing forward prices.
- There are two general categories of trades distinguished by how they "settle" at the delivery period:
  - Physical trades: The commodity is delivered in a specified fashion by the seller to the buyer; the buyer pays cash to the seller at the confirmed transaction price.
  - Financial trades: Only cash is exchanged—the seller pays the buyer a published settlement price ; the buyer pays the seller the confirmed transaction price.

We will go into much more detail on trade mechanics and valuation in later chapters. We will conclude here with a description of how trading desks are typically organized.

The Composition of the Trading Desk

Natural gas trading shops often have to deal with *many* distinct risks. For every delivery location there is a spot price, as well as forward prices for each delivery month. Simple arithmetic illustrates the point. A typical trading desk with reasonably complete coverage of the U.S. will have trades at several dozen individual delivery locations—say 30, for our purpose here. The tenor of the portfolio, that is how far into the future forward trading has occurred, varies by delivery location, but a conservative estimate would be several years of forward exposure—say, for example, three years. Then the number of forward prices relevant to the operation is 30x36 or 1080 prices.

Add to this the spot prices and the number becomes 1110. Even if many of these prices are closely coupled, there are still a lot of prices to track.

To effectively handle this high dimensional risk profile, trading desks are usually organized in something of a divide-and-conquer fashion, with regional desks dedicated to sets of risks that are closely related due to infrastructure coupling. A useful way to understand a trading operation is to follow the life-cycle of a trade, which we will assume here to be physical.

Consider the situation in which on 01Apr2016 the desk sells 10,000 MMBtus per day for the entire year of 2017 ("Cal 17") for physical delivery at TETM3. The price of the sale is $2.75/MMBtu. Recall that this is a delivery location in the northeastern U.S. for which spot prices were shown in Figure 3.1. The price is roughly 12 cents / MMBtu above the mid-market price on that date—this is to pay for the activities of the groups below and the associated transaction costs involved in hedging.

- Origination

Trades like this can and do occur directly between traders or between traders and exchanges. However, often commodities shops have a group dedicated to client interaction. While effectively a sales force, this activity is often given the more glamorous name of "origination". In the example above, a northeast natural gas originator may have brought the deal to the trading desk via a conversation with a local utility in the area. Origination groups can be organized by client, so that each company with whom the shop does business has a single point of contact in the group. However, coverage is more commonly organized geographically. Regional coverage is advantageous for several reasons—among them specialization of knowledge of local regulations, idiosyncratic market structure and political forces, as well as more efficient travel requirements in the course of client visits and contract negotiation. Finally, it fits more naturally into the regional organization of the traders.

- Regional Desks

Upon execution, any transaction immediately resides in the portfolio of a trading desk which is responsible for the risk management of the trade and its ultimate performance. The trading group is, therefore, usually responsible for pricing—in our example, deciding on the price at which to offer the natural gas to the customer. Much like origination, trading desks are usually organized regionally, with the TETM3 sale usually under the auspices of the "Northeast" desk.

Regional desks are themselves usually organized according to the tenor of the risk:

- Term traders: These are the trader(s) responsible for positions at longer delivery periods (relative to the current date). Often this encompasses all risk positions except for the current month, also referred to as the cash month.
- Cash traders: The trader(s) responsible for managing the set of trades with delivery during the cash month.
- Schedulers: The trader(s) responsible for managing the immediate delivery of physically settling trades.

In our working example, delivery starts well into the future at the time of the trade, and hence is under the purview of the term traders. Handoff of this trade to the cash trader will occur at or near January 2017, where this single month of physical exposure will be transferred to the cash desk. The term trader will continue to manage the trade from February on out, until of course when February "goes cash." The cash desk handles the intra-month price exposures. Each day the scheduler deals with the arcane and detailed tasks required to ensure physical delivery of the natural gas to the utility on the other side of the trade.

- Exchange Desk

As things stand, it would seem that our sample trade has been handled from origination to delivery. However, there is an important additional aspect to the way that most natural gas desks are organized. The regional desks typically rely heavily on the exchange desk—the trader(s) who focus exclusively on the Henry Hub market. The importance of this activity is due to the fact that Henry Hub is the "benchmark" for U.S. natural gas markets[13].

If the regional traders focused solely upon their niche locational markets, liquidity would be diffused. Instead, largely as a tradition arising from natural gas infrastructure near the Gulf of Mexico, Henry Hub is the liquidity center for natural gas trading in the U.S.—it is the benchmark. There is more trading activity at Henry Hub than at other locations, both in the sense of higher trading volumes and liquidity of longer tenor contracts. As we will see in later chapters, natural gas prices tend to move broadly in tandem, at least at long tenors and over the time scales of hours and days. These two facts, namely that liquidity is concentrated at Henry Hub and that natural gas prices tend to move together over short periods of time, renders the benchmark extremely useful.

Returning to our transaction, when a sale of natural gas for delivery at TETM3 over one year is transacted, it is highly likely that the very next action taken would be for the term trader to hedge this position by buying natural gas at Henry Hub. The liquidity at Henry Hub renders this routine—it can be done more or less instantly. Since all of the regional desks would handle trades in this way, benchmark Henry Hub trading is usually centralized. The exchange traders who handle this flow play a pivotal role on the desk as they are the conduits for large volumes of benchmark hedging activity.

The physical organization of a trading floor often reflects this structure,

---

13 The term benchmark is a term that is broadly used in all markets, from bond traders on fixed income desks to commodities desks, referring to key tradable instruments that by market consensus are highly liquid.

with the exchange traders at the center and regional clusters of traders and originators around it. The central role of the exchange desk for the entire group does not mean that the exchange traders are the desk "masterminds." Rather, they are specialists at moving large volumes of risk through the benchmark futures contract. The regional desks arguably have the more challenging responsibilities, having to track vast amounts of detailed locational information to handle the specific risks in their respective portfolios. The organizational structure is pragmatic, minimizing execution costs and netting through an exchange desk before facing the outside world.

The organization of trading desks mirrors the liquidity hierarchy in the markets, with the benchmark Henry Hub contract at the apex of liquidity absorbing large components of the price risk being hedged by end users. Not all trading desks are organized in exactly this way, but most resemble this structure at least in part. The purpose of the remaining chapters is to put substantive detail around each of these activities—the actions that traders take and what motivates them.

PART II

Market Drivers

Introduction

In this second section we delve into more detail on the factors that affect natural gas price dynamics. This will include the way in which the attributes of physical infrastructure and observable fundamental variables such as weather and inventory levels impact prices. In Chapter 4 we begin with the drivers of supply and demand. This will include evolving production and consumption patterns as well as the role of natural gas storage in balancing temporal mismatches between supply and demand. Loosely speaking, the topics in Chapter 4 directly affect price levels.

In Chapter 5 we turn to factors that primarily affect price spreads—differences in prices for natural gas at different delivery times or at different delivery locations. This will involve a more detailed discussion of natural gas storage, which moves natural gas through time, and pipelines, which transports natural gas between locations.

CHAPTER 4

Supply and Demand

THE PRIMARY PURPOSE of a deregulated energy market is to provide a reliable mechanism for setting spot prices so that supply and demand balance. The way that spot prices behave is, therefore, directly related to the factors that affect relative levels of supply and demand. As we will see here, for natural gas changes in supply can be large over long time scales, but on short time scales supply is relatively predictable. Variations in rate of production are largely responsible for long term trends in price levels. In contrast, demand fluctuations typically arise from variations in weather and can, therefore, be large and rapid. Changes in demand tend to drive short term price movements.

There are always exceptions to such heuristics. Compressor failures on pipelines can instantly cause a drop in supply at a particular location, thereby causing short term price spikes. Relocation of fertilizer production overseas, which can take months or years, is an example of systematic long term changes in demand. An additional complication is the role of storage. Natural gas held in inventory can, often at the discretion of its owners, be used to generate either additional supply or demand at short notice. If you have gas in storage you can create additional supply by withdrawing it and selling it into the spot market. If you have empty storage capacity you can create additional demand by purchasing natural gas and injecting it into storage. In North America the amount of storage capacity is large enough to materially alter "natural" levels of supply and demand, thereby affecting price dynamics.

In this chapter we will discuss the primary factors affecting supply and demand of natural gas—the drivers of absolute price level. In the next chapter we turn to the factors that primarily affect spreads—transportation and storage.

Broad Trends

Figure 4.1 shows both annual U.S. gross production and consumption.

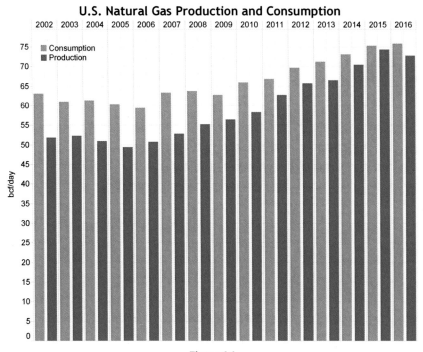

Figure 4.1

Domestic annual consumption has consistently exceeded production over this period. Things clearly changed around 2005 when production started to increase. Up to that point the consensus view was that U.S. production would continue to fall, a result of declining production of aging fields, particularly those in the Gulf of Mexico. In the mid-2000s unconventional production methods began to accelerate, quickly reversing this trend and ultimately significantly narrowing the supply deficit.

The increase in production relative to consumption has resulted in a marked drop in prices. Figure 4.2 shows daily natural gas spot prices at Henry Hub, in addition to a 250 trading day moving average[14] which reduces the effects of daily volatility and seasonality.

---

14 A centered Gaussian moving-average was employed here.

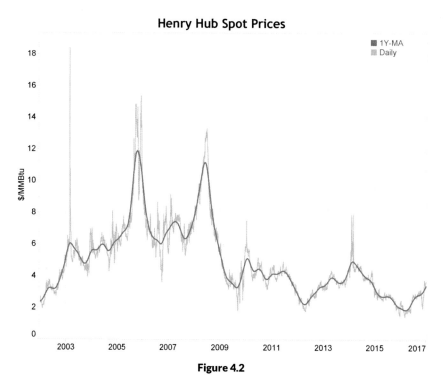

Figure 4.2

Comparing these two figures, the secular drop in prices starts more or less contemporaneously with the change in production and provides a striking example of the effects of long time-scale supply changes.

Production

The first stage of the commodities life-cycle is shown in 4.3 in the form of monthly U.S. production. Current dry (we will talk about this term later) production levels slightly exceeded 75 bcf/day in 2015, before falling back to around 70 bcf/day at the end of 2016. This recent decrease was the result of lower prices for both natural gas and crude oil.

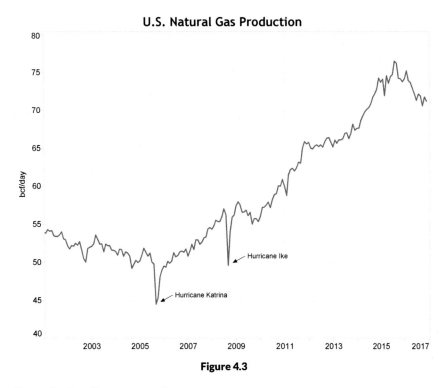

Figure 4.3

Several other features stand out.

First, the impact of two severe hurricane events are clearly visible. Drops in production in the face of a hurricane are typically the result of precaution rather than of outright damage to infrastructure. When a hurricane impact is imminent, rigs are evacuated and wells are "shut in" resulting in a reduced production, even if it turns out that the realized damage is minimal. Hurricanes in the Atlantic typically occur in the June to November time-frame, the so-called "hurricane season." A second noteworthy feature is the secular rise in production starting in the middle of the 2000s due to "unconventional" methods of extraction to which we will turn shortly. Finally, while extremely cold weather can impact production due to freezing wellheads and pipelines through "freeze-offs", there is no obvious seasonality to production. Changes in production tend to be slow, with long term trends superimposed on relatively small fluctuations, aside from the occasional hurricane.

- Reserves

Oil and gas producers spend vast sums of money each year in the quest for new reserves—property rights with access to an extractable resource. Reserves can be either proven or unproven—the distinction between the two categories being somewhat qualitative in nature. Proven reserves are deemed to be available for extraction with high probability at prevailing market prices using current technology and under the existing regulatory framework. Unproven reserves are those for which the potential economic merits of the resource are less certain.

The EIA periodically publishes estimates for proven dry natural gas reserves as shown in Figure 4.4. Reserves at the end of 2015 exceeded 350,000 bcf, an increase of nearly 70% from 2005, a consequence of shale gas discoveries. This volume corresponds to roughly 15 years of consumption, and as of the end of 2015 unconventional sources, primarily shale, constituted the majority of U.S. reserves.

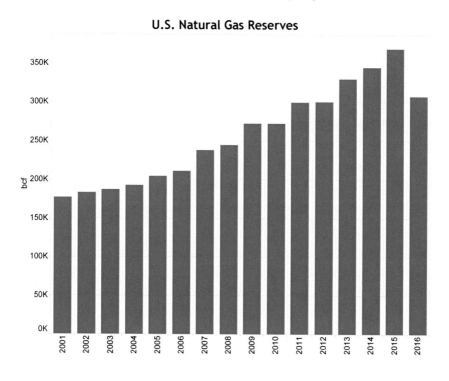

U.S. Natural Gas Reserves

Figure 4.4

- Exploration

In order to produce natural gas, you need to find it. The search for reserves is referred to as exploration. Exploration involves a preliminary assessment of geological structures of interest, often using seismic technology. Fleets of drilling rigs of various types are then deployed to potentially viable areas to locate and ultimately extract natural gas.

The oldest form of drilling rigs currently in use are vertical rigs, named such as they bore vertically from the surface. Vertical rigs drill straight down; they cannot change direction or drill sideways. More sophisticated methods have long been in use, notably directional drilling and slant drilling, which provide additional degrees of freedom in the relationship between the locations of the reservoir and the rig.

A milestone in drilling technology occurred with the advent of horizontal drilling rigs, first pioneered early in the 1980's, but only significantly gaining traction in the mid-2000s. Horizontal drilling involves drilling a standard vertical bore to a desired depth, followed by drilling horizontally in multiple directions. Horizontal drilling avails an entire stratum of a geological structure to a single well, dramatically increasing the efficiency of exploration efforts since a single rig can probe much more territory. This technology plays a central role in shale fields, which requires extraction from thin rock formations. Horizontal drilling and hydraulic fracturing together have been the technological underpinnings of the shale gas revolution.

Exploration results in production, and production impacts prices. There is often (but not always) a direct feedback of prices to the exploration process—lower prices should reduce the incentive to explore. The number of rigs which are active at any given time, the rig count, is a commonly discussed statistic as many consider it to be a leading indicator of future production and, therefore, price changes. Figure 4.5 shows the weekly count by type of rig.

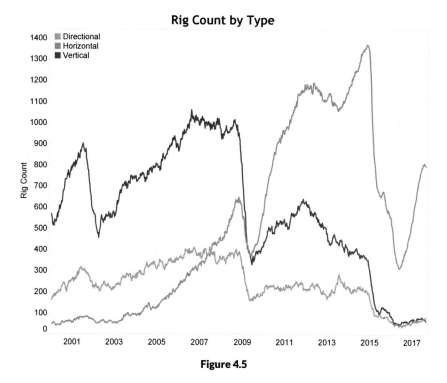

Figure 4.5

The growth in horizontal drilling stands out clearly, as does the immediate drop in drilling activity at the inception of the credit crisis and for some period thereafter.

Although rig count continues to mesmerize market participants, it is not clear that it is a particularly useful statistic from a trading perspective. Figure 4.6 shows total rig count with Henry Hub prompt month prices superimposed.

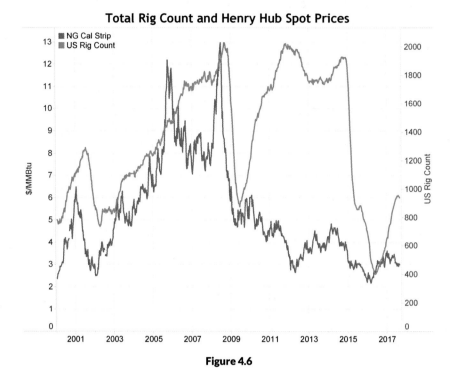

Total Rig Count and Henry Hub Spot Prices

Figure 4.6

If anything, large price drops seem to *precede* drops in rig count, as seen in both 2001 and 2008. Moreover, meaningful price changes have occurred at other times without any apparent relationship to rig count. The rig count increase starting in 2009 resulted in the shale gas supply glut, but the price response has been slow and difficult to predict.

There are reasons that rig count and prices may only be loosely correlated. Rig count is one step removed from the setting of market prices: production responds to rig count, and price responds to production, not to mention demand and inventory level. In addition, improvements in rig technology means that newer rigs are more efficient than older ones, endowing the rig count statistics with an inherent non-stationarity. Complicating matters further is the fact that drilling is not always followed immediately by production.

Many wells are now categorized as "drilled but uncompleted" or DUCs for short. The DUC count, shown in Figure 4.7,

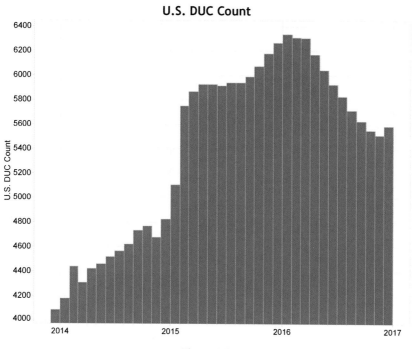

U.S. DUC Count

Figure 4.7

was incidental prior to 2014. In recent years, however, the number has risen to a level that has become relevant. Shale gas production is a two-step process. The first step is for the producer to drill the well to desired specifications. The second step is to frack the well and extract the gas. A DUC is a well that has been drilled, but not fracked. These distinct steps usually involve two different teams and the time required for teams to arrive and complete work inevitably results in the existence of some DUCs. But there is more going on here. The fracking process costs money and once completed it is usually optimal to begin production immediately. If prices are low the owners may consider delaying the fracking stage in anticipation of potentially higher prices. Moreover, in some instances "use it or lose it" lease provisions, discussed a bit more shortly, can stipulate that wells have to be drilled, but not necessarily pushed to completion with fracking and the assembly of gathering systems.

The punchline is that evolving technology and the strategies of each producer make rig count a challenging statistic to apply in practice.

- Extraction

Natural gas is found in underground deposits which can either be on land or under the ocean floor. Production is usually grouped as follows (EIA) (Nat):

- Associated Production: This is natural gas which is derived from wells that are primarily producing crude oil—the production is "associated" with crude oil production.

- Non-associated Production: This type of production arises from underground reservoirs with no crude oil; the primary purpose of the well is the production of natural gas. Non-associated production yields so called "dry gas", namely natural gas from which liquids have been extracted. Non-associated wells are the primary source of natural gas production in North America.

- Gas Condensate: This is natural gas which is best thought of as non-associated natural gas, but in which the extracted product contains enough in the way of additional heavier hydrocarbons, such as ethane, propane, isobutane and butane to warrant attention. These non-methane products are referred to as natural gas liquids, or simply NGLs.

Natural gas that is rich in NGLs is referred to as "wet gas". When wet gas is pumped out of a well, it is a mixture of both hydrocarbon and non-hydrocarbon gases, although methane is usually the primary component. By the time it reaches market it is almost pure methane. The removal of impurities and other hydrocarbons, referred to as "stripping", is the conversion element of the life cycle discussed in Chapter 2. NGLs have value in their own right, being commonly used in the industrial production of plastics as well as alternative sources of energy (see the insert at the end of this chapter). The prices of the NGLs are typically coupled closely with the prices of natural gas and crude oil; a coupling that, as we will see shortly, has some interesting consequences.

In cases where it is not economic to transport and market associated natural gas, it is often simply burned ("flared") so as not to create a nuisance. Flaring occurs when a producer must dispose of natural gas due to the absence of viable economic alternatives, and is more common for newer oil production fields for which natural gas gathering systems have yet to be constructed. For example, in Bakken Fields in North Dakota in May 2014, drillers were reported to have flared as much as 33% of their associated natural gas (Platts, 2014). This seemingly pointless combustion may appear wasteful and destructive from an environmental perspective. However, the resulting carbon dioxide has a much lower greenhouse footprint than does methane; if the natural gas is not going to be collected and used, flaring is preferable to outright release.

Production is also categorized as either conventional or unconventional, the former referring to production from non-associated and gas condensate wells—the "traditional" sources of production. Unconventional production is extracted through a set of relatively new technologies that allow extraction of natural gas that is trapped in porous geological structures. There are three common sources for unconventional production (EIA):

- Coalbed methane: Methane that is trapped in coalbeds migrates with water. If the water pressure is reduced at some point in a coal seam, water flows in the direction of the pressure gradient, taking the gas with it. Coalbed extraction gained traction in the early 2000s and is considered to be the first significant unconventional method of natural gas production.
- Tight gas: Some dense rock formations hold trapped natural gas, extraction of which typically requires more energy than other forms of unconventional production. Most tight gas production occurs in the Rockies.
- Shale gas: Natural gas is also found in some shale rock formations. Extraction involves hydraulic fracturing, or more commonly "fracking", in which a slurry consisting of water and an assortment of chemicals

and sand is injected into wells at very high pressure, fracturing the surrounding rock and releasing the gas.

- Production Profiles

All forms of production rely upon pressure gradients which pull natural gas toward the point of extraction. In conventional wells these gradients arise both from geological forces (natural gas deep beneath the seabed is typically at high pressure) and from pumps which pull gas to the surface. As natural gas is extracted, natural pressure gradients decrease, and the rate of production slows during the lifetime of a well. This trajectory of production is referred to as the production profile and the rate at which production decreases is called the decline rate. In the absence of technological innovation, the incremental cost of extraction from a well will ultimately rise to a point where production is not economical, at which point the well is retired. Conventional wells usually have production profiles that decline over the time scale of several years, although decline rates can vary widely both among fields and between individual wells.

Unconventional methods rely upon human-induced pressure gradients and alterations to naturally occurring geological structures. There is relatively limited historical production data for unconventional wells, at least in comparison to conventional wells. Shale production is generally thought to have relatively high initial production rates, followed by fast decline rates. The replacement rate for shale gas, which is the rate at which new wells must be drilled to keep overall field production rates flat, is higher than for conventional wells. The amount of natural gas that is ultimately recoverable from shale fields is not clear, and estimates made by both private and public-sector sources vary widely.

- Recent Surplus

By 2010 unconventional production was dominated by shale gas. While fracking remains controversial, the production boom has been nothing short of astonishing and is the primary driver for the price decoupling shown in Figure 2.2. One would expect production to fall as markets search for a new equilibrium in the face of continuing weak prices, but this has been slow to happen for several reasons.

One reason is that shale producers tend to hedge the value of future production using futures contracts (the way in which this is done is, in fact, a central topic in the subsequent chapters). For the duration of such hedges, producers are in effect insulated from the economic consequences of low spot prices. (Economist, 2017).

Another factor is the "use it or lose it" structural market convention embedded in many land leases. Such provisions motivate production, even in the face of adverse prices, and from the point of view of the individual land owners seem to make perfect sense—the land owners want royalties from production. Collectively, however, the result can be a supply glut and, in the long run, painfully low prices for both producers and land owners alike.

Finally, the dubious notion of "first mover advantage" has, at least until recently, contributed to excess production. Well into the price drop, equity investors continued to buy into the notion that early investment had inherent benefits, with profitability relegated to a longer-term goal. Only recently have low prices started to dampen producer enthusiasm, although even at the time of writing, with several years of consistently low prices, production remains remarkably high.

There is another factor contributing to the surplus—NGLs provide what can be thought of as a "market subsidy" for production. Figure 4.8 shows the daily spot price for propane versus the first WTI futures price from Jan2007 to Aug2015. Relatively high oil prices, at least in comparison to natural gas, have been reflected in commensurately high NGL prices.

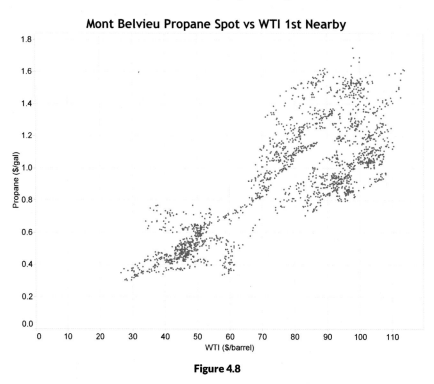

Figure 4.8

High NGL prices helped to maintain the profitability of natural gas with high NGL content—so called wet gas. Strong NGL prices lower the break-even production price for wet gas, at times pushing it below the market price of natural gas. This phenomenon has likely contributed to the decoupling of natural gas and crude oil prices in the past decade. A drop in oil prices would typically cause a drop in NGL pricing and, therefore, a bias toward reduced natural gas production and increased natural gas prices.

- Changing Views

Prior to the shale gas boom the prevailing belief was that domestic production, which was concentrated in the Gulf of Mexico, would continue a systematic decline. LNG imports to the U.S. would, it was believed, be the primary mechanism for relieving supply shortages. At the time it was hard to envision the current situation where supply growth seems likely to continue for the foreseeable future. Figure 4.9 shows historical production as well as long term production forecasts provided by the EIA[15].

Natural Gas Production by Source
1990-2040

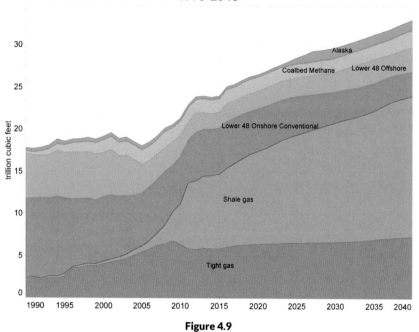

Figure 4.9

Unconventional production grew from inconsequential volumes in 2005 to well over half of the total production at present. The prevailing view is that shale gas will completely dominate supply in the upcoming decades.

Markets that function properly ultimately find new equilibria after large perturbations. As we will see later in this chapter, LNG exports are increasing and many believe that LNG will unify disparate regional markets, rendering natural gas as global in nature as crude oil. All such prognostications should, however, be taken with a degree of skepticism. The future is hard to

---

15 This forecast was published in 2011; more recent forecast show a similar theme

predict—in 2000 the prevailing view was one of decreasing production and increasing dependence on imports; fast forward ten years and this seems a naive, almost quaint perspective. New technologies could result in equally dramatic changes. Moreover, the regulatory environment is always a wild card. The environmental impacts of fracking are a continued source of concern, as is the increasing frequency and size of earthquake clusters in proximity to fracking activity. Fluctuations in the global economic and political landscape can also change the viability of international LNG flows. All of these factors could result in future supply being very different from what we think it is going to be now.

Consumption

Total U.S. annual consumption of natural gas in 2016 was just under 29 tcf (trillion cubic feet) or roughly 76 bcf/day. Consumption is discussed in terms of the following categories:

- Residential: Household usage, which is predominantly related to home heating.
- Commercial: Non-manufacturing businesses.
- Industrial: Usually large manufacturers. This category includes producers of petrochemicals and fertilizers.
- Generation: Demand arising from electricity generation.
- Pipelines: Natural gas consumed in the process of transport and storage.
- Vehicles: The small but slowly growing fleet of natural gas fueled transportation.

The average annual consumption of each category is shown in Figure 4.10.

U.S. Natural Gas Consumption by Category

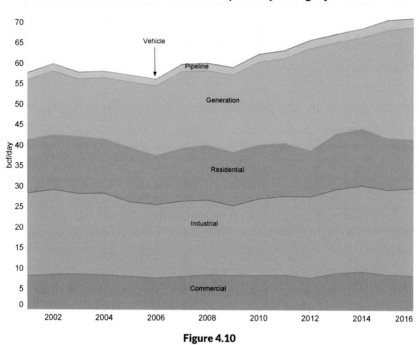

Figure 4.10

The evolution of demand in the two largest categories, electricity generation (utility) and industrial usage, are particularly interesting.

- Generation

Electricity generation increasingly relies on natural gas as a fuel source. Natural gas has several advantages over other fossil fuels, a fact that we touched on briefly in Chapter 2. In comparison to coal and oil, natural gas combustion yields much lower rates of emission per unit of heat produced—this includes both carbon dioxide and nitrous oxides. Moreover, natural gas generation yields almost no sulfur dioxide, mercury or particulates associated with comparable coal generation.

Figure 4.11 shows the relative contributions of energy sources to the Electricity sector.

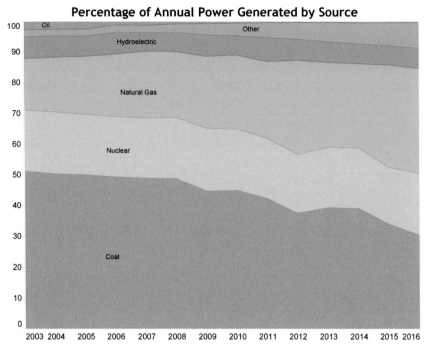

Figure 4.11

In 2016 natural gas captured the lead with a roughly 34% footprint; coal was second place at 30%. Ten years earlier coal had the edge at roughly 50% in comparison to 20% for natural gas. There are two primary reasons for this trend. First, the efficiency of combined cycle generation has consistently increased over the years, with the amount of natural gas required per unit of electricity easily 10% lower than a decade ago. The second reason is falling natural gas prices.

For many years coal was markedly less expensive than natural gas per unit energy, but this historical price advantage has eroded as natural gas prices have fallen. Figure 4.12 compares the price of coal, converted to an approximate cost per MMBtu, with that of natural gas[16]. The change in the relative

---

16 Conversion of two commodity prices to comparables is almost always replete with simplifying assumptions. Here we assumed that Central Appalachian coal yielded 25 MMBtu of heat, required $25/ton to transport and sustained $1/ton of emissions costs. These assumptions are purely to obtain a reasonable qualitative assessment of the relative value of the two fuels. Transportation costs depend on where your generator is, as does the cost of natural gas. Moreover, although Central App is definitely a coal benchmark, many other types of coal are available with varying chemical compositions which affect heat content and emissions, as well as transport costs.

costs of the two fuels remains the primary driver for the continuing migration to gas-fired generation.

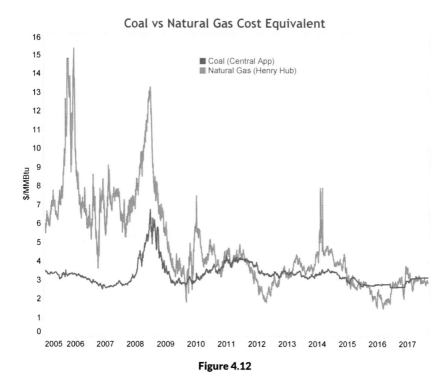

Figure 4.12

- Industrial Consumption

Industrial usage is interesting not only due to the fact that it is the second largest demand category, but also because industrials exhibit notable price elasticity. A close look at Figure 4.10 shows that industrial demand decreased in the mid-2000s even while global economies were (ostensibly) strong. The main driver for this demand destruction was the roughly four-fold increase in natural gas prices between 2000 and 2006, which provided a strong incentive for companies to move industrial demand overseas when possible. High prices from 2005 through mid-2008 caused, or at least contributed to, a drop in industrial usage of over 10% from 2002. This trend has reversed in recent years as prices have fallen.

Although manufacturing processes are not rearranged globally due merely to a single month or two of price fluctuations, industrial usage is price dependent. If forward curves imply years of uncompetitive pricing, some industrial companies can and do relocate to lower price venues. The Manufacturing Energy Consumption Survey (MECS), sponsored by the department of Energy and released every four years, provides some insights into which types of activities are price sensitive.

Figure 4.13 shows total industrial usage in addition to that of the chemicals industry, which is by far the largest component of the subsectors.

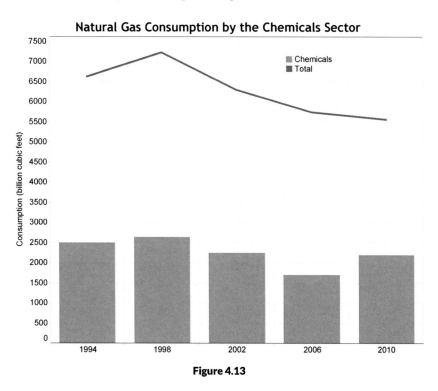

Figure 4.13

U.S. chemical companies tend to be more exposed to natural gas prices than their international counterparts, as they rely more on NGLs obtained from crude oil. Roughly 85% of ethylene (a hydrocarbon gas with many commercial uses, including the production of plastics) production in the U.S. uses NGLs derived from natural gas feedstock, while in Western Europe approximately 70% is derived from oil products (O'Reilley, 2011). This explains the sensitivity of U.S. petrochemical demand, and the roughly 25% drop between 2002 and 2006 when prices were rising rapidly. More recently the secular drop in natural gas prices has resulted in a return of some previously expatriated activities, and demand from the chemical sector is expected to continue to grow.

- *Consumption Dynamics on Short Time Scales*

Up to now we have focused on long term trends in consumption. However, shorter time-scale behavior is both interesting and complex, and a primary factor in the high level of spot price volatility.

Demand is highly seasonal. Figure 4.14 shows U.S. monthly consumption and gross production.

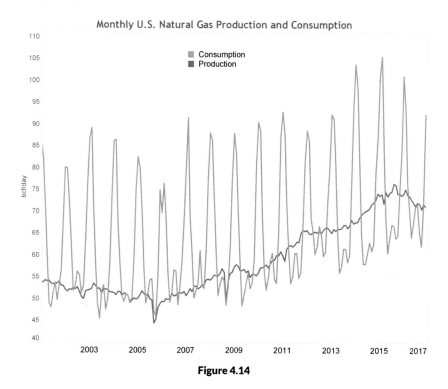

Figure 4.14

Note the high winter peaks and the relatively mild summer peaks in consumption, the latter due to electricity demand arising from air-conditioning. Consumption varies dramatically on such short time scales due to weather.

Rapid variation in demand coupled with slowly varying, non-seasonal production results in huge imbalances on short time scales. This mismatch is resolved by natural gas storage. Figure 4.15 shows working natural gas inventory as published by the EIA on a weekly basis.

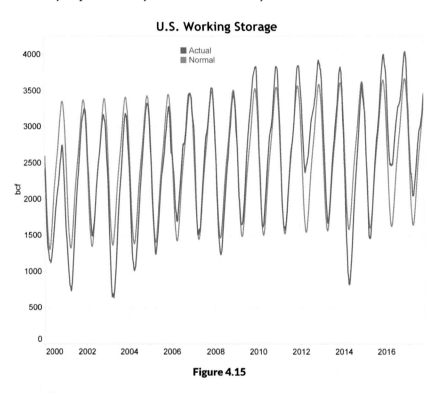

Figure 4.15

We will discuss storage in more detail later, but for now working inventory should be thought of as the amount of natural gas in storage that is readily available for withdrawal. The key feature of the inventory level is the seasonal response to the supply/demand mismatch, with injection during the summer months in anticipation of withdrawal during the winter. The remarkable drop in inventory near the end of the series was due to the "polar vortex" winter of 2013-14. At the time of writing, another period of extremely low temperatures is likely to result in similar drops in inventory.

Inventory level impacts forward prices and conversely, making the "storage number" as it is called one of the most discussed statistics on natural gas trading desks. For commodities without obvious seasonality, such as copper, it is abso-lute level of inventory that matters. For seasonal commodities such as natural gas, with the obvious annual cycling, absolute level matters primarily when stor-age is so full or so empty that the limits of storage capacity are being tested. Most of the time, however, this is not the case, and the question on everyone's minds is how current levels of inventory compare to where one would expect them to be at that point of the injection / withdrawal cycle. The most relevant metric is, therefore, where inventory is versus "normal" levels at that time of the year.

Defining what normal means involves not merely adjusting for the season-ality in Figure 4.15, but also accounting for changes in total working storage capacity, as new storage facilities are added. Another complicating matter is that nobody knows exactly how much natural gas could be withdrawn if absolutely required. Most estimates put the total working storage capacity in the U.S. at or near 4.4 trillion cubic feet as of 2016—roughly one sixth of annual consumption. There is, however, considerable uncertainty and debate about this number.

Many commodities research teams define normal inventory using somewhat arbitrary historical averages by time of year; often the five-year average is used. There is merit to the simplicity of this metric—it is easy to understand and to validate; but there are also weaknesses. A few aberrantly cold winters or an extra hurricane or two, as well as additions to storage capacity can dis-tort the estimate of normal inventory meaningfully. The results of a some-what more sophisticated (and we believe reliable) approach are shown in the second series appearing in Figure 4.15. The methodology used is intended both to avoid overfitting and to include capacity additions.[17] The departure

---

17 This estimate of normal storage levels used EIA estimates for total storage capacity by year to con-struct a linear capacity growth of about 20 bcf/year during this period. The de-trended inventory series was then fit with a Fourier series, the number of modes selected using an out-of-sample forecasting criterion. The resulting expected storage $\bar{S}(t)$ is of the functional form:

$$\bar{S}(t) = \alpha + \beta t + \sum_{k=1}^{K} \left[\gamma_k \sin\left(2\pi kt\right) + \delta_k \cos\left(2\pi kt\right) \right]$$

with t measured in units of years, and where the parameters $\left[\alpha, \beta, \gamma, \delta\right]$ are estimated using linear regres-sion. Out-of-sample selection methods yield K=2 as the optimal number of modes.

of inventory from normal levels: $R(t) = S(t) - \overline{S}(t)$, which we will refer to as the storage residual, is shown in Figure 4.16.

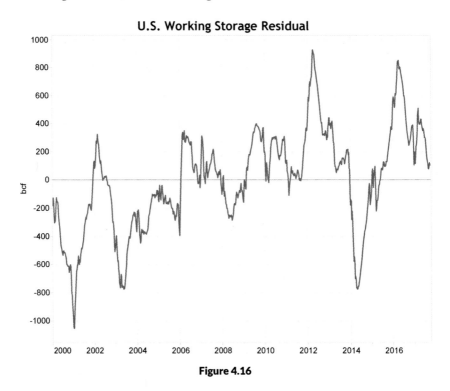

Figure 4.16

Once again, the draw-down during the polar vortex stands out. In addition, the data suggest that increased production is systematically pushing inventory levels higher. Later we will see how the departure of storage from normal impacts prices.

Weather is the most important short-term driver for demand. The large drop in inventory seen in early 2014 was a direct result of the infamous polar vortex. Figure 4.17 emphasizes this point by showing the weekly change in inventory scattered against daily average temperature at LaGuardia Airport in New York City from 2000 to 2016.

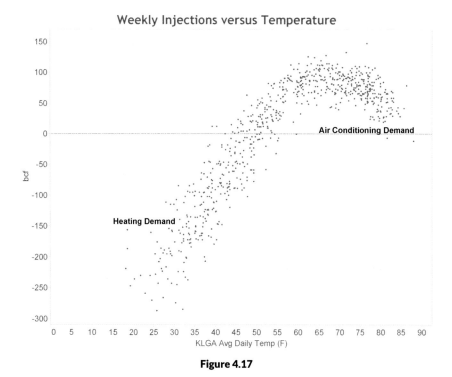

Figure 4.17

Cold temperatures increase heating demand, which necessitates withdrawal of natural gas from storage. The drop in injection rates at high temperatures is due to air conditioning demand.

It is possible to build models of this behavior with an array of temperature data from around the country. Many trading desks do just that, adding other variables and detailed data on pipe flows to attempt to predict the weekly change in inventory—all in an effort to obtain a short-term trading advantage. However, while short term variations in demand are relatively predictable, longer time-scale trends are a different matter. The impacts of macroeconomic events such as the credit crisis, trade policy, industrial demand elasticity, as well as technological innovations like the deployment of combined cycle generation, were all very difficult to anticipate with any degree of precision.

Imports and Exports

We conclude our survey of supply and demand by turning to flows into and out of the U.S. and North America. Historically imports into the U.S. from Canada dominated all other flows. The other land based market bordering the U.S. is of course Mexico, although so far volumes have been relatively small. LNG has played a relatively minor role to date, but this is changing due to expanding facilities and relatively low domestic prices.

- Canada and Mexico

The U.S. and Canadian natural gas markets are tightly coupled by pipelines. In fact, the AECO trading hub in Alberta, a benchmark Canadian delivery location, often trades as a spread to Henry Hub. Figure 4.18 shows the spot prices of AECO hub and Henry Hub in units of $/MMBtu with AECO exchange rate converted.

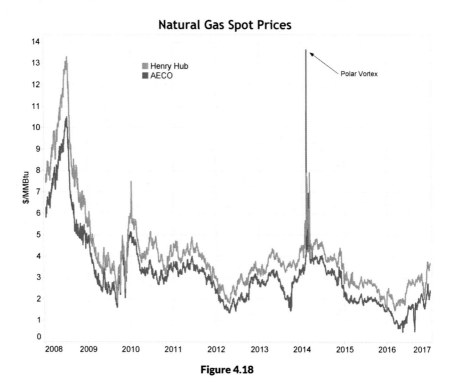

Figure 4.18

These prices are clearly coupled. The systematic discount of AECO prices to Henry Hub is the driver of Canadian exports. In 2001 the U.S. imported 9.8 bcf/day from Canada, representing roughly 15% of the total consumption that year. In 2006 the U.S. imported about 8.9 bcf/day, which was an almost identical fraction of total usage. By 2016 Canadian imports had dropped to slightly under 6 bcf/day corresponding to approximately 8% of total consumption. In short, Canada is becoming less relevant to U.S. natural gas markets.

The story with Mexico is almost exactly the opposite. Natural gas flows with Mexico have been more or less a rounding number in the greater scheme of things, but with recent increases in demand and new pipeline projects, Mexico is poised to become a relevant factor in the supply and demand balance. In 2009, U.S. exports to Mexico were approximately 0.8 bcf/day. Contrast this to 2014 in which the U.S. exported approximately 2 bcf/day; while in 2016 the figure was just under 4 bcf/day. Although still small relative to total U.S. production, the trend is toward increasingly significant volumes.

- LNG

Liquefied natural gas (LNG) is the only way to transport natural gas globally in significant quantities[18]. The concept is simple—cool natural gas until it is in a liquid state, load it onto specially designed ships, which can keep it cold, and upon arrival let it become a gas again. But the process is expensive due to the substantial infrastructure and the energy required to cool natural gas to liquid form and to keep cold over the course of weeks at sea.

Liquefaction facilities chill natural gas to below $-160°C$, at which point the liquid methane is loaded onto LNG transport ships. Upon arrival regasification terminals, also referred to as "send-out" facilities, increase the temperature thereby returning the natural gas to usable gaseous state. Development

---

18 Compressed natural gas (CNG) remains a developing technology but it is unlikely that CNG will develop a large footprint in global transport in the foreseeable future.

costs, while difficult to estimate, are large. Liquefaction facilities typically cost on the order of $2b to $5b per one bcf/day of capacity; regasification facilities are cheaper at roughly $500m for the same capacity. Figure 4.19 shows major regasification facilities in North America .

LNG Terminals

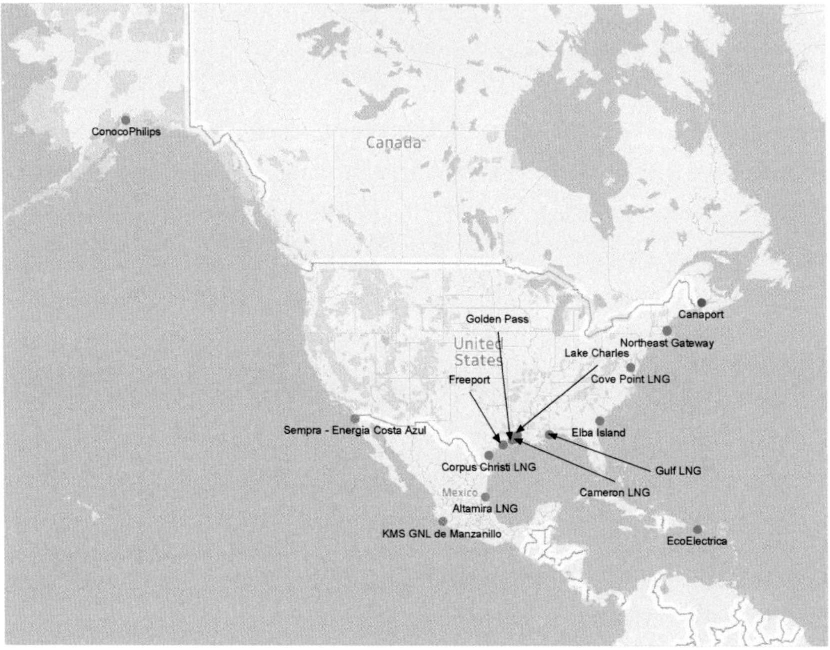

Figure 4.19

Building infrastructure is a fixed cost. Once built, however, price differentials are exploitable only insofar as they exceed the costs to move the commodity from the discount location to the premium location. For LNG transport these costs are significant. Liquefication is energy intensive, and shipping costs depend on the distance the cargo needs to travel. The Center of Energy Economics (CEE) at the University of Texas (Foss, 2012) made the following estimation of LNG transport costs in 2012 in $/MMBtu:

- Liquefaction: $0.90 to $1.30.
- Shipping: $0.50 to $1.80 depending on shipping distance.
- Regasification: $0.40 to $0.60.

If we assume a Henry Hub price of $3.00, transport to the liquefaction ter-
minal of $0.25, a cost of $1 for liquefaction, the total cost of LNG on the
vessel is $4.25. With additional shipping costs of $1 and a further $0.50 for
regasification, the delivered costs becomes $5.75 per MMBtu.

For comparison, Figure 4.20 shows historical spot (or first contract month)
prices at the Henry Hub and the National Balancing Point in the UK, as well
as an index estimate of the LNG import price for Japan. All series have been
converted to $/MMBtu adjusted for exchange rates.

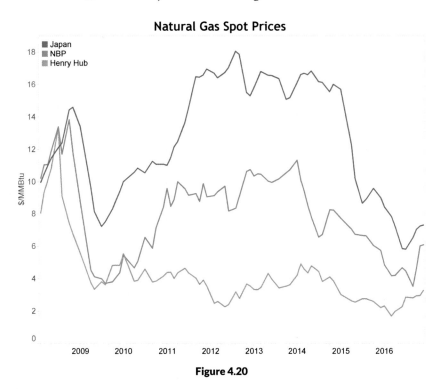

Figure 4.20

Export to Japan is typically supported by these price differentials; to Britain
(NBP) the situation is marginal as spreads have compressed[19].

_____

19 One factor driving international spreads is that some international gas markets have traditionally
indexed pricing to crude oil. The contemporaneous (and partially related) drop in oil prices has compressed spreads between international and U.S. prices. At lower oil prices the transport costs become a
larger component of the delivered product, rendering the ostensibly low U.S natural gas prices at times
only marginally competitive in international markets.

Figure 4.21 shows annual rates of LNG imports and exports in bcf/day, with 2017 a partial year with data available through July.

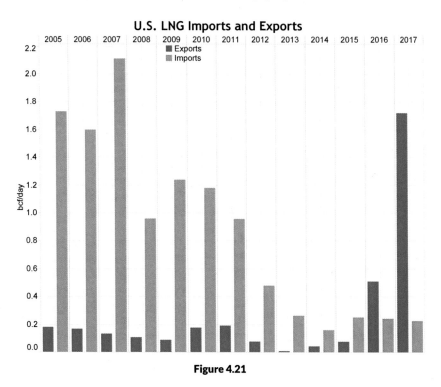

Figure 4.21

The appetite for imports has waned, and as LNG export facilities have come online, the rate of exports has increased[20]. It is important to note the scale on this plot—current rates are under 2 bcf/day. On one hand, this seems small in comparison to typical consumption of over 70 bcf/day. However, as we saw in Figure 2.8, regional imbalances are in the ballpark of 10 bcf/day for the Middle East and Asia; for the U.S. the imbalances are much smaller. From this perspective 2 bcf/day in exports is a bigger deal. The growth in U.S. exports is likely to continue with additional LNG export permitting and development.

---

20 For years regulations have slowed the development of export capacity. The topic of energy security has been a sensitive subject for Americans from the time of the oil crisis in the 1970s. The Natural Gas Act (NGA) prohibits export of natural gas without the approval of the Department of Energy (DOE). High levels of production and low domestic prices, however, have rendered the DOE increasingly amenable to granting such approvals.

CHAPTER 5

Storage And Transport

Where a commodity is produced is generally not where it is consumed. Most people don't live near a natural gas fracking field. The same is true for *when* a commodity is produced. Natural gas production is reasonably uniform throughout the year, but people need it most in the winter. Pipelines and increasingly LNG handle the "where" part, moving natural gas from producing fields to high consumption areas. Storage handles the "when" part of the requirement; injecting and withdrawing from storage balances supply and demand across time.

The infrastructure required to move and store natural gas is expensive to build. Much as for telecom networks or electricity transmission, equal access to key infrastructure is necessary for a competitive marketplace to exist. Due to their inherent nature as monopolies, owners of pipelines and storage are regulated via tariff structures to ensure open access and equitable pricing for all market participants. We will discuss some basic facts about storage and pipelines before returning to pricing and operations.

Storage

Production rates of natural gas tend to change slowly with time, in contrast to seasonal demand which can vary wildly day to day. Storage capacity resolves this temporal mismatch. We saw in Figure 4.17 that weekly deficits in excess of 200 bcf occur routinely in the winter months, driven by short time-scale fluctuations in temperature. Over a single month this can result in deficits in excess of 500 bcf above and beyond production. Large volumes of natural gas must be stored each summer to accommodate the high demand of the following winter, and some of this storage has to be able to respond quickly to sudden changes in demand.

One way you could imagine handling this is by liquefying natural gas, reducing volumes by orders of magnitude. As we saw earlier, however, LNG is a very energy intensive process. It is far more economical to utilize geological structures to hold the large volumes required.

- Storage Capacity

As of 2016 the EIA estimates that the U.S. has a total storage capacity slightly in excess of 9200 bcf. The major storage facilities that comprise this capacity are shown in Figure 5.1.

Major U.S. Storage Facilities.

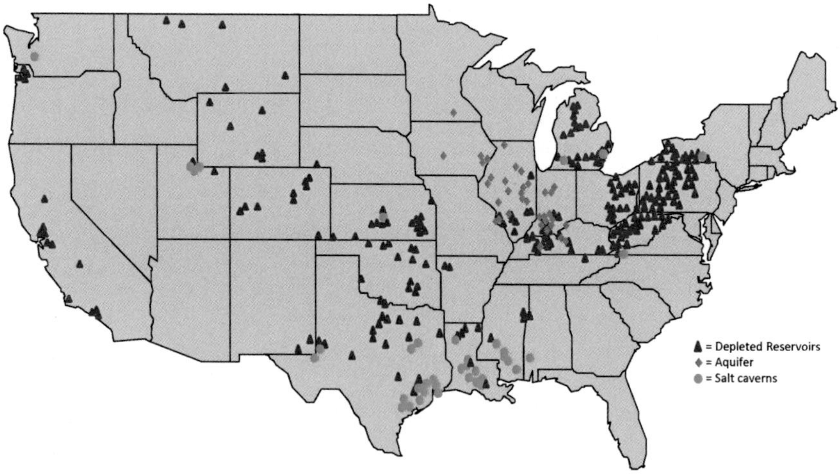

Figure 5.1

Storage is concentrated in the Gulf and Northeast United States. There is also a cluster of facilities in the Canadian provinces of Alberta and Saskatchewan.

The total "nameplate" storage capacity of 9200 bcf is deceptively large. Roughly 4400 bcf of this capacity holds so-called "base gas" or "cushion gas". Base gas is the natural gas required for a storage facility to maintain operational pressure. Think of base gas as the minimum level of inventory below which withdrawal is not practical; it is effectively not recoverable. The U.S. has, in theory anyway, roughly 4800 bcf of storage capacity in the sense that we usually think about it. This remaining capacity is called "working storage".

The statistics above sound deceptively precise, and in fact mask a considerable uncertainty regarding how much working storage actually exists. No one really knows just how high or low inventory can go before injection or withdrawal becomes infeasible. Exactly what these limits are is routinely debated at industry conferences and publications. The only way to establish these limits with certainty is to actually hit the limit—this has not happened yet.

Figure 4.15 provides some information, but only roughly as facilities have been added and retired along the way. One statistic that is useful, however, is the demonstrated maximum working gas volume of 4,373 as reported by the EIA for November 2016. This number corresponds to the sum of the non-coincident maxima of reported storage volumes of the 385 working storage facilities in the lower 48 U.S. states[21]. It is reasonable to believe that at least this amount of natural gas, which corresponds to roughly 15% of total annual demand, could be stored if required.

---

21 The result stated here is the sum of the maximum reported storage volumes achieved by each facility from December 2010 through November 2015.

- Types of Storage

The detailed physical attributes of a storage facility are quite complex. There are, however, several aspects of natural gas storage facilities that are important to understand.

Geological storage facilities are categorized as follows.

- Aquifers: Natural aquifers are porous rock structures modified to serve as gas storage reservoirs. Aquifer storage is located primarily in the Midwest.
- Reservoirs: Some depleted natural gas and oil production fields can be modified to accept injections. Reservoir storage is most common in the Northeast.
- Salt caverns: Salt dome formations can be engineered for gas storage. Of the three types of storage, these are the closest to resembling large tanks. Salt cavern storage has relatively high rates of injection and withdrawal, which is particularly useful at accommodating rapid changes in demand. Found predominantly in the Gulf states, salt cavern storage can deliver roughly 35% of total daily withdrawals, even though it comprises under 10% of total working storage (EIA).

The difference between the relatively small capacity footprint and the high impact of salt cavern storage leads us to the concept of cycling rate. The cycling rate is the time required to fill and then empty a storage facility—this refers to working gas only. Cycling rates are usually discussed in terms of the number of times a facility could be turned (filled and emptied) in one year— or in the vernacular, "turns per year."

Aquifer and reservoir storage are usually cycled once per year. This puts them in the category of base load storage—storage used primarily to balance the long time-scale seasonal variations in average demand. Salt cavern storage, in contrast, can cycle several times per year; usually two or three turns

annually, though in some cases as high as six or seven. High
ties, also referred to as peak load storage, are used to accomm
weather-driven variations (EIA) (Nat). Cycling rate is a high
statistic that depends on the engineering attributes of storage. ...,
rough guide to the type of storage facility being discussed and what one can
expect in the way of performance. The faster the facility can cycle, the more
valuable it is per unit of storage capacity. Table 5.1 summarizes general attributes of the three storage types.[EW03].

Type	Base to Working	Injection (days)	Withdrawal (days)
Aquifer	50% - 80%	120 - 200 days	60 - 120 days
Reservoirs	$\approx 50\%$	120 - 200 days	60 - 120 days
Salt cavern	20% - 30%	20 days	5 - 20 days

Table 5.1: Natural Gas Storage Attributes by Type

- Constraints on Storage Facilities

The rate at which you can pull from storage depends on the pressure of
the gas being stored. The pressure differential between the facility and wellhead is what pushes natural gas out of a storage facility. At high pressures
withdrawal rates are greater than at low pressures—the less there is in the
container the harder it is to access what remains. Conversely, the rate at
which gas can be injected decreases with inventory level. As storage gets full,
it becomes harder to push more in. To complicate matters further, aquifer
storage is particularly sensitive to injection and withdrawal patterns. If either
injection or withdrawal are done too quickly, spatial variations in pressure
can reduce maximum rates. How fast you pushed gas in or pulled gas out in
the recent past affects what you can do at the present time.

The key point is that injection and withdrawal rates depend on inventory
level. The spot price response to a high demand day in the winter in the

Northeast, for example, should be affected by the amount of natural gas in inventory, with more dramatic spikes to be expected if inventory levels are low. Conversely, if inventory levels are high then injection rates during summer months will be lower than normal, resulting in weaker spot prices.

Another common type of constraint applies directly to inventory levels. Many storage facilities require that inventory be at-or-below or at-or-above defined levels at specified times. These limits are called ratchets. For example, aquifers and reservoirs are often constrained to end the withdrawal season with appropriately low inventory—a rule of thumb being that at least 35% of the storage volume carried into the winter season must be withdrawn by the next injection season. Each storage facility has its own geological and operational constraints, and the engineering purpose of ratchets is to ensure optimal performance. Cycling natural gas into and out of the reservoir minimizes the migration of gas to areas of the geological structure that are not accessible. Migration reduces the quantity of base gas supporting the facility's operation. If too little cycling occurs, and inventory is left sitting in storage for long periods of time, the storage facility loses natural gas and replacing it costs the storage owner money. Such leakage always occurs to some degree, but cycling reduces the losses.

Ratchets are also viewed as potentially impacting spot price behavior. High inventory levels near the end of the withdrawal season can be potentially bearish for cash prices since ratchets can force owners of stored natural gas to withdraw it and sell it into the spot market.

We will see later that inventory levels affect forward prices, and conversely forward prices affect the actions of storage owners. Storage couples prices across time. We turn next to transport, in which pipelines couple prices at different delivery locations.

Transport

In a perfect world commodities would be produced at or near where they are consumed. In some cases this fortuitous situation is a reality. When a coal-fired generator is sited near a coal mine, the fuel source is both more dependable and much cheaper than if it is delivered by rail. Solar panels on rooftops are another example in which production occurs at the location of the consumer.

This idyllic situation does not tend to occur in natural gas markets. From inception the U.S. natural gas markets have developed in tandem with an elaborate and evolving pipeline system that moves wellhead gas to consumers.

- The Pipeline System

The life-cycle of natural gas starts at the wellhead from where it is transported to processing facilities that remove non-methane components. Short-haul pipelines then take the gas to one of the long-haul pipelines in the system shown in the map produced by Bloomberg in Figure 5.2.

North American Pipelines (Bloomberg)

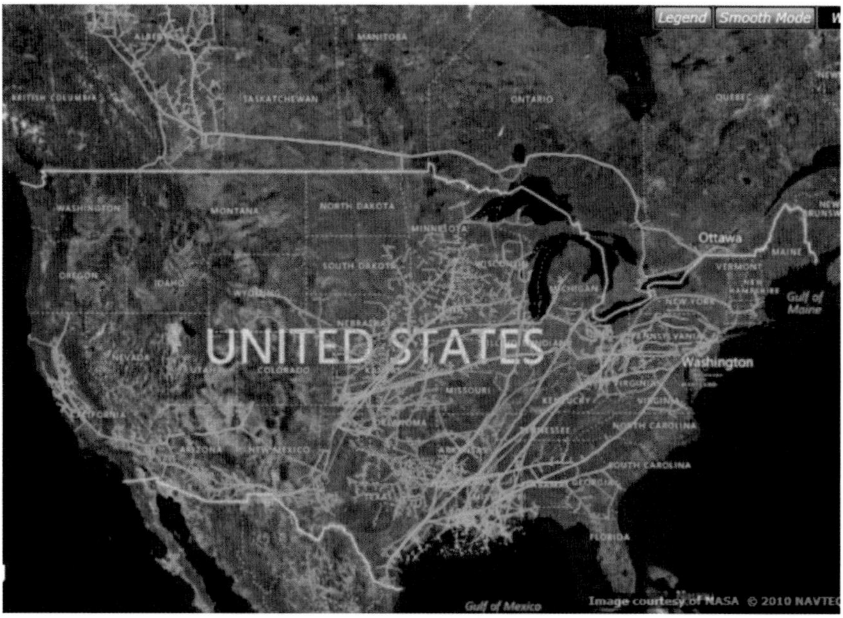

Figure 5.2

At the "sink" (the demand side of the pipeline) natural gas is delivered to city-gates. Here local distribution companies (LDCs) are responsible for the final delivery to retail end-users. At the city-gates, or along the way via lateral pipelines, gas is also delivered to large industrial users and electricity generators.

The pipeline network shown is comprised of over 300,000 miles of pipes in the continental United States. The concentration of pipelines in Figure 5.2 is consistent with the general layout of supply and demand centers. The system initially evolved to bring natural gas from the conventional producing areas, both onshore and offshore in the Gulf coast, as well as the Rockies and Canada, to the demand centers in Northeast and the Midwest.

- Shale Gas and Changing Production Patterns

The pipeline system is anything but static. Existing pipelines are constantly being expanded to handle a growing demand, and new pipelines are built to accommodate changing patterns of production and consumption. When too much gas is produced in a location relative to available transport capacity, prices drop in the area increasing the economic incentive to find a way to move the gas to demand centers where prices are higher.

In recent years shale gas production has changed not only total U.S. production rates, but it has also dramatically altered the geographic distribution of production. Figure 5.3 shows the major U.S. shale producing regions (or shale plays, as they are called).

Major U.S. Shale Plays

Figure 5.3

Of particular note is the Northeastern Marcellus play which has completely upended the natural gas basis markets.

Figure 5.4 compares the relative contributions of the top producing U.S. states, as well as the aggregate of the other lesser contributors, in 2010 and 2014.

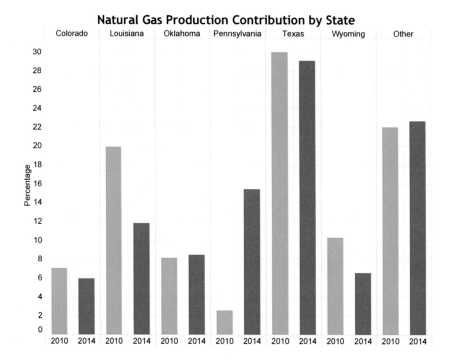

Figure 5.4

The impact of Marcellus production is clear in the difference reported in Pennsylvania. Major changes in the pipeline network were inevitable in the face of changes of this magnitude. The traditional producing areas prior to 2010 generally required transport into the Northeast and Midwest from the Southeast and Rockies areas. In contrast, markedly higher Northeast production has reduced these flows, if not at times outright reversing them, spawning the need for new pipeline capacity.

Until recently U.S. natural gas markets were typically viewed in terms of three regions.

- The Gulf, or producing region, so named for natural gas production in the Gulf of Mexico and the substantial infrastructure located in the Gulf states. This is the reason that the NYMEX NG contract references Henry Hub in Louisiana.

- The East: The states east of the Mississippi river, excluding Gulf states.
- The West: States west of the Mississippi river.

Through 2015 the weekly EIA storage numbers were reported in terms of these regions. In this pre-shale gas era, the dominant pipeline flows were from the Gulf and the Rockies to the high heating demand regions in the Midwest and Northeast, consistent with the general pipeline layout seen in Figure 5.2.

Shale production changed things. The EIA now reports storage numbers using five regions—Figure 5.5 contrasts the two reporting regimens.

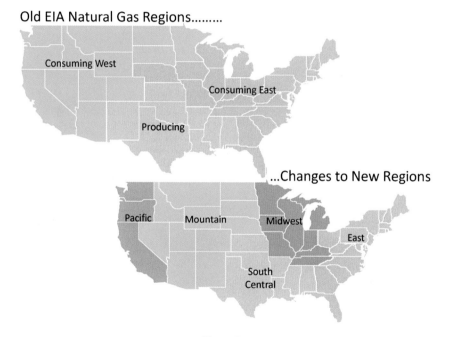

Figure 5.5

The dominant pipeline flows have also been affected. The excess supply in the Marcellus region has resulted in flows to the higher demand centers further east and west, in addition to flows toward the Gulf in warmer months. Insert 5.1 at the end of this chapter surveys some of the major pipelines most commonly discussed on trading desks, as well as some of the recent changes.

We turn next to costs associated with pipeline and storage capacity.

Tariffs

The U.S. pipeline system is the most extensive in the world. Building it required (and continues to require) large amounts of capital; investments with time horizons often spanning many decades. The funding requirements for this effort were initially met by state-owned energy companies or privately held vertically integrated utilities regulated by government agencies. Eventually, the concept that competition would yield more efficient capital allocation gained traction, spawning an era of deregulation that began in the 1990s.

Pipeline and storage owners have a natural monopoly in the areas in which they operate. For a competitive marketplace to flourish, rules must be in place to ensure access to essential infrastructure. This requires a regulatory framework which ensures that pipeline companies earn a viable return for building and operating pipelines and storage, while protecting end-users from potential monopolistic abuse.

The primary regulatory mechanism to achieve these complementary goals is the tariff. A tariff is a defined pricing and access protocol to specified infrastructure, typically designed in collaboration with market participants and asset owners, and ultimately approved by regulatory agencies. State regulators oversee intrastate pipelines, while interstate pipelines are regulated by the FERC. According to the National Gas Act, all pipelines under FERC jurisdiction must charge rates that are "just and reasonable". The FERC determines what rates of return are, in its view, consistent with achieving required pipeline investment.(FERC) Moreover, the FERC is under legal obligation to set rates of return that will allow the pipeline companies to continue to attract capital and maintain their financial integrity. For more details, see Appendix A. Storage facilities are regulated and covered under the same tariffs as pipelines, and inherit the same regulatory framework. Facilities connected to interstate pipelines are regulated by the FERC, while those associated with intrastate pipelines or local distribution companies (LDCs) are subject to state regulation.

Tariffs effectively set upper bounds on the prices that pipeline companies can charge customers for transport and storage. Moreover, as set forth in the Natural Gas Act, interstate pipeline capacity must be availed to the highest bidder, up to the maximum rate defined in the tariff. This free market principle of "highest price wins" prevents storage and pipeline operators from allocating capacity to favored customers, such as unregulated merchant trading arms of their own holding companies.

- Types of Transport

The types of services that pipelines can offer are also regulated by the FERC. In general, pipelines offer two broad categories of transport service:

- Interruptible capacity: Owners of interruptible capacity can have their transport capacity reduced on short notice for a variety of reasons ranging from compressor problems, pipeline rupture or emergency maintenance. If you own interruptible storage, you will have the ability to transport during "normal" operating conditions, but if things go wrong you can experience reductions in your ability to move natural gas on the pipeline.
- Firm capacity: Owners of firm capacity have priority over interruptible capacity. Transport cannot be disrupted unless there is an event of force majeure[22] that cannot be resolved by total reduction of all interruptible capacity.

Clearly, interruptible capacity is less expensive than firm capacity. Also, in practice things are not as simple as implied by these two classes of storage. Most pipelines offer a spectrum of transport categories with varying degrees of reliability, with the details varying by pipeline.

---

22 Force majeure refers to an unforeseeable or unavoidable event beyond the control of the entity responsible for delivery of a service or commodity.

- Buying Pipeline Transport

The cost to procure transport is typically comprised of three components.

- Capacity payment: This is usually a fixed monthly payment for the term of the contract. This payment is made regardless of the amount of natural gas transported, and should be thought of as the cost to own the option to transport—an option premium of sorts.
- Fuel charge: The second component is a fuel charge, which is volumetric and which can depend on the transport distance. A fuel charge can be a fixed amount per unit notional, for example $0.05 per MMBtu; or a volumetric charge such as 1% of the gas transported, which is economically equivalent to 1% of the spot price at the source. The fuel charge is intended to fund the cost of running the compressors and to cover fuel losses.
- Annual charge adjustment: The FERC also allows pipelines to charge their customers a percentage of the total value of the gas transported in order to recover the annual charges assessed to the pipeline by the FERC. These charges cover the costs to pay for FERC administration charges. (FERC, 2011).

As an example, suppose you have purchased one-contract per day of pipeline capacity from the beginning of April to the end of the following March at a cost of $1.50/MMBtu for capacity, a fuel charge of $0.05/MMBtu, and an annual charge adjustment of $0.0014/MMBtu. If in a given month you ship 20 contracts, then your payment to the pipeline consists of the sum of $15,000 (the product of the capacity cost and the daily capacity of 10,000) and $10,280 (the product of the sum of the fuel charge and the ACA charge with the volume of 200,000 MMBtus of total notional transported). Had circumstances arisen where you had no economic reason to ship at all during the month, the only cost you would pay is the $15,000 capacity payment.

Pipeline and storage capacity are typically bought and sold in one of two ways. The first is via a request for proposals (RFP). In situations in which a pipeline company is expanding capacity, extending a pipeline, or simply selling existing capacity for a future time period, an RFP may be announced, the purpose being to solicit bids from market participants for the capacity. RFPs are typically for unusual or large transactions. The second type of transaction is via the electronic bulletin board (EBB). The EBB is a platform in which asset owners can offer transportation or storage capacity into the marketplace, and can be thought of as akin to any internet based sales platform. Anyone interested in acquiring pipeline capacity can monitor capacity releases on the EBB and bid on such at their discretion.

Physical Operations

The mechanics of moving and storing natural gas on the physical system are somewhat complex. This section is not central to the broader themes and can be skipped without loss of continuity.

At some point in time after transport or storage capacity has been procured, gas molecules need to flow. This is the domain of the schedulers on natural gas trading desks. Scheduling is the process in which the movement of physical molecules is arranged between counterparties on a specific pipeline. Schedulers are the face of the trading desk to the pipelines and are responsible for any issues relating to physical flow, and as such they are in a unique position to glean information from other participants regarding flows, potential constraints on the pipeline and planned maintenance. Such information can be quite useful to both cash and term traders.

- Scheduling Cycles

Scheduling activities occur on a portal that is accessed through the pipeline's EBB. The unit of time over which natural gas is scheduled and delivered is the "gas day" (GD). The GD starts at 9:00 am CST and continues to 8:59am CST on the next calendar day[23].

---

23 The gas day is not a calendar day, which results in an annoying mismatch with closely related electricity markets that function on calendar days. This results in generators having to nominate and schedule for two gas days just to handle a single calendar day of generation.

The process of scheduling for next GD delivery is typically divided into four cycles[24].

- Timely cycle: In this first cycle, market participants must have their physical gas flows scheduled (nominated) before cash trading ceases at 13:00 CST for the next day.
- Evening cycle: Corrections of errors in nominations or entirely new nominations resulting from trades executed after the timely cycle can be made during the evening cycle, which ends usually at 6 pm CST on the night prior to the flow date.
- Intraday cycles: On the delivery day the scheduler needs to check and confirm the flows. If additional modifications are required these are made during the "intraday" cycles. In general, intraday nominations can be used to increase or decrease natural gas flow, but original nominations cannot be completely deleted due to the fact that scheduled gas has already flowed—a flow volume is usually calculated by prorating the scheduled quantity up to the time of the contemplated change. There are usually three intraday cycles: ID1, ending at 10:00 CST of the day of the flow; ID2, which ends at 14:30 CST; and ID3, which ends at 19:00 CST.

On the face of it, this scheduling protocol may seem arcane and needlessly scripted. However, the physical delivery of a commodity is not comparable to the wiring of funds or title to securities. The system has to handle demand spikes or infrastructure problems which were not anticipated a day earlier, and at present the cycles are the mechanism for doing so.

- *Cuts and Balancing*

Most market participants are exposed, in one way or another, to the unpredictable nature of the infrastructure as well as to human or systems errors. As a consequence, there is generally good will in attempting to resolve unanticipated changes to scheduled flows.

---

24 The number of cycles can vary by pipeline, but four is typical.

Frequently, cuts are resolved by an agreement to make up the cut volume on a later date or even to simply change the volume on the original trade. Things can get messy, however. If one of your counterparties cannot take delivery of the full volume that you were supposed to deliver, then you may have to cut deliveries that you take from your suppliers. This results in ripple effects throughout the supply chain. Changing the volume on a trade can lead to the entire "daisy chain" of market participants having to make changes. Whenever possible, schedulers try to localize these perturbations to maintain orderly markets and reduce administrative headaches.

As a practical meter it is very difficult for each customer to precisely estimate the exact quantity of natural gas that it will consume during a day. After each flow day most will have imbalances—variations from quantities originally nominated. Small imbalances can be maintained and accrued, provided that the total imbalance remains within operating rules of the pipeline. Some pipelines will charge for these imbalances, while others simply permit resolution (true-ups) with the pipeline itself. For large and highly variable demand, such as electricity generation, Operating Balancing Agreements (OBA) are commonly in place with the pipeline, which specify protocols for daily long and short balances as well as a cumulative rolling balance.

- The Transport Hierarchy Revisited

It is useful to revisit the concept of firm transport from the perspective of scheduling. Firm transport has priority over interruptible transport. A caveat, however, is that firm transport is only actually firm when the nominated flows are between the primary receipt point and primary delivery point that was specified when the transport capacity was purchased. Any variations to receipt and delivery points are not firm. Even flows that are nominated between meters that are geographically spanned by the primary points, which one might logically assume would be considered firm, do not have firm transport status.

Another way in which firm transport can be degraded to interruptible is to nominate the flow after the timely scheduling deadline. Such flows are no longer firm, and are demoted to a lower status. What owners of firm transport can lose will in some cases benefit owners of interruptible transport. As discussed earlier, interruptible nominations only flow when capacity is available above and beyond firm transport requirements. However, during the flow date, there is a "no-bump rule" on the pipelines, which states that after the ID1 cycle, firm transport nominations cannot preempt (or bump) interruptible transport. This can complicate the operations of electricity generators who often are then forced to nominate gas flows well in advance of knowing their actual fuel requirements, which can vary hourly.

Insert 5.1: The Major Pipelines

Pipelines are usually grouped by geographical region, in much the same way that trading desks are organized.

Gulf to Northeast

The primary transport corridor in the U.S. from the Gulf to the demand centers in the Northeast is dominated by four pipelines:

- Columbia Gas Transmission: The CGT pipeline operates about 12,000 miles of pipelines across 16 states with capacity of approximately 3 bcf/day and 660 bcf of storage
- Transco: The Transco pipeline network consists of roughly 10,200 miles of transport from Texas and Louisiana to the Northeast, notably New York City. Its peak capacity is about 10.9 bcf/day and has roughly 200 bcf of associated storage.
- Texas Eastern (TETCO): TETCO is comprised of 9,200 miles of pipelines capacity of roughly 11 bcf/day accompanied with 75 bcf of storage capacity. The TETCO system transports gas from south Texas and

Louisiana across most of the eastern half of the country, ultimately connecting to the Algonquin system in New Jersey.

- Tennessee (TGP): Tennessee has roughly 12,000 miles of pipeline primarily from Texas and Louisiana to the Northeast supplying in particular New York City and Boston.

Gulf to Midwest

Transport from the Gulf to the Midwest is the second significant transport corridor. Of note are:

- Natural Gas Pipelines (NGPL): NGPL serves the Midwest area with gas from Texas with a network of over 9,200 miles of pipelines with roughly 290 bcf of associated storage.
- Panhandle: This network sources gas from Oklahoma and Texas and transports it through a system of 6,000 miles and a capacity of 2.8 bcf/ day to their customers in Illinois, Indiana and Michigan.
- ANR: With roughly 10,000 miles and just under 300 bcf of storage ANR is one of the larger systems in the Midwest. The primary customers are the states around Lake Michigan with sourcing split in two legs: the south west leg taking the gas from Oklahoma and the southeast leg from Louisiana.

Between West and East

There are several other smaller but important transportation corridors that support the changing production patterns in recent years. These include:

- Rockies Express (REX): This is the most recently built major interstate pipeline, having become fully operational in 2009. REX was built to alleviate the excess supply in the Rockies, a region which had been sustaining spot prices well below $1/MMBtu. REX is the only major pipeline that crosses the U.S. laterally from West to East, transporting

Rockies gas to major markets through the Midwest to eastern Ohio. It has close to 1,700 miles of pipe and has a throughput of 1.8 bcf/day. As of 2015 REX can also transport from eastern to western locations.

- El Paso: This pipeline system consists of roughly 10,200 miles of pipe, moving gas from Permian basin in west Texas and Oklahoma to southern California at a capacity of roughly 5.6 bcf/day.

Canada

Finally, the U.S. imports roughly 10% of its daily consumption of natural gas from Canada primarily through:

- Transcanada: This pipeline system stretches from the AECO market in Alberta in the west to the eastern part of Quebec connecting at the U.S. border at several points along the way. The network consists of 26,000 miles of pipes and 130 bcf of storage in Canada.
- Alliance: The Alliance pipeline brings gas from north eastern British Columbia and north western Alberta into the Chicago market on roughly 2,300 miles of pipeline at a throughput of 1.6 bcf/day.

Mexico

As discussed in Chapter 4, exports to Mexico have become increasingly important. Two major pipeline systems are:

- NET Mexico: This is a 120 mile, 2.3 bcf/day Texas intrastate pipeline delivering gas to Mexico at a point near Rio Grande City, TX. NET is currently the largest shipper of U.S. natural gas into Mexico.
- North Baja: This is a 220 mile, 0.5 bcf/day pipeline that crosses the California border into Baja California connecting to the TGN pipeline in Mexico.

PART III
Natural Gas Trading

Introduction

WE TURN NEXT to the trading of natural gas, with a focus on the motivations of market participants to trade in the first place.

In Chapter 6 we start with what we refer to as price level trading—the outright purchase or sale of natural gas. This will require development of the important concepts of forward curves, futures markets and the basics terms of trade. Market liquidity is concentrated at the so called benchmarks—those price locations that by historical convention have the greatest level of trading activity and the most transparent pricing. In this chapter we will focus on trading activity using the benchmark Henry Hub contracts.

Time spreads are the topic of Chapter 7. These involve the simultaneous purchase and sale of natural gas at two distinct future delivery times. In addition to trade mechanics and relationships between time spreads and storage, we will also cover the practical application of time spreads to hedging long term positions.

Chapter 8 covers the other type of spread on which we will focus—namely locational or "basis" trading. Just as storage is central to time spreads, pipelines are the infrastructure that underpins basis risk.

Finally, in Chapter 9 we conclude by discussing natural gas options and commonly transacted hedging structures.

Along the way various technical sections appear in framed text—these can be skipped without impact on subsequent material.

CHAPTER 6

Price Level Trading

MOST MARKET PARTICIPANTS are thinking about price risks over delivery horizons spanning months and years into the future. This is especially true of the natural longs, the producers who are actively hedging price exposures over several years, often at the behest of their shareholders. Natural shorts, both the retailers which sell to end-users and large industrial consumers, are usually focused on shorter time horizons, but they still typically manage price risk a year or two into the future.

This means that most trading in natural gas occurs "out the curve", and the forward curve should be thought of as the source of risk and the primary object of interest. As we will see shortly the dominant movement of forward curves is when all prices move up or down in tandem. Secondary effects are the changes in the spreads between forward prices at different tenors. These statements, which can be made mathematically precise, serve to organize the next two chapters. Here we will focus on hedging the first dominant movement which we refer to as price level risk. In the next chapter we will turn to the trading of time spreads.

Benchmarks

Trading in most asset classes, including natural gas, revolves around benchmarks, a term that we have already used casually on a few occasions. The term benchmark refers to a tradable instrument in which there is a very high level of liquidity and the price of which is commonly agreed upon as a reference for other similar, but less liquid instruments. Benchmarks facilitate the trading of larger notional quantities than would be possible if liquidity was diffused across all delivery locations and products.

Most asset classes have some form of benchmark. In treasury bond markets, for example, positions in less liquid ("off-the-run") bonds will often be hedged using the more liquid recent issuances ("on-the-runs) or bond futures. The same is true for equities where ETFs and index products can be used to quickly hedge closely related risks, and for credit markets where investment grade and high yield CDX indices serve a similar purpose. For energy markets the most commonly discussed benchmarks are the WTI and Brent futures, which serve as benchmarks for crude oil and refined products more broadly.

North American natural gas markets use the Henry Hub futures contract as the benchmark. Hedging of most natural gas price risk across North America starts with Henry Hub futures, which at settlement requires the delivery of natural gas at Henry Hub in Louisiana. Although the shale gas revolution has resulted in high levels of production and delivery far from this delivery location, the Henry Hub contract has been the benchmark from inception of the modern U.S. natural gas markets and will likely remain so for the foreseeable future.

Most of what follows will focus on the use of the benchmark in trading. First though, we will start by elaborating on some basic concepts and terminology which we have already touched upon briefly.

Spot Prices

The spot price of a commodity is the price for "immediate" delivery. There are always delays between agreement to transact and actual flow of molecules. In natural gas trading the concept of immediate delivery usually refers to physical delivery of MMBtus tomorrow, or more precisely on the next business day. Figure 6.1 shows a spot price series for natural gas at Henry Hub. This is a daily series—the price is plotted as a function of the delivery day, so each price was established on the prior business day.

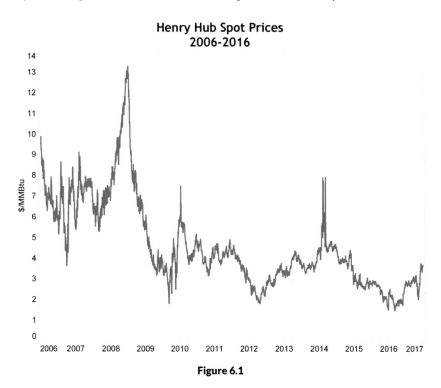

Figure 6.1

Throughout the prior business day trades can be occurring bilaterally between all manner of different counterparties at various (though probably quite similar) prices. Spot price indices like the one shown here are usually established by survey. In this case Bloomberg, the source of this index, surveys participants in the physical gas markets and constructs a volumetrically weighted average price for delivery at Henry Hub on the next business day. Similar indices are calculated at a large array of delivery locations. Platts is another provider of such indices, trademarked as "Gas Daily" indices which are commonly referenced in trade confirms.

How much trading was occurring during any particular day clearly matters. At liquid trading points the sample size of available trades from which to calculate the average is large. In less liquid locations, however, there may be very limited transactional data, and the price surveys conducted by reporting services should be thought of as little more than rough indications of what prevailing prices may have been. At some locations and on some days, there can be no available price data whatsoever, rendering the concept of a spot price rather moot.

Daily spot price series serve several purposes. First, they are informative, providing everyone from traders to policy makers an estimate of the price of natural gas on a daily basis. Second, and arguably more importantly, these prices serve as indices for trade settlement. There are two key points to keep in mind:

- When people talk about "the spot price" they are usually referring to published indices that are intended to represent the average transaction price during the trading day. These indices are commonly used in the settlement of financial trades.
- When you are buying or selling physical gas, the "spot price" you actually experience is whatever price you manage to negotiate for your transaction. This price will in general be different, in theory by a small amount, from the spot price index that is published for that day.

Forward Contracts

While spot (or cash) trading is where the "rubber hits the road", most of the action on trading desks occurs in the forward markets. Commodities "trade forward", meaning that in most transactions a buyer agrees to purchase from a seller a commodity at a fixed price, mutually agreed upon by both parties, for delivery at a specified time in the future. In a forward trade you agree now to a price for the commodity to be paid at a specified delivery time in the future. Forwards, as well as closely related futures, earn their names because you agree to a price now for forward delivery.

In Chapter 3 we introduced the concept of the forward curve, which is the set of prices "now" for various delivery times in the future. As an example, Figure 6.2 shows the benchmark natural gas forward curve for delivery at Henry Hub, LA as things stood at the end of the trading day on 07Mar2016.

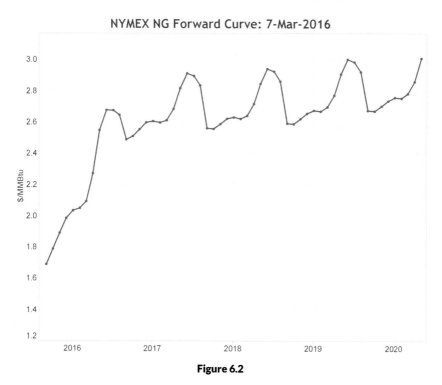

Figure 6.2

Each point on the curve corresponds to the price for delivery of natural gas during the corresponding calendar month as of this particular trading date. For example, on 07Mar2016 you could buy or sell natural gas for delivery in Jan2017 at a price of $2.677 (this is the value shown corresponding to Jan17 on the x-axis), up to a bid/offer spread. If you did purchase natural gas at this price and engaged in no subsequent trading then in Jan2017 you would receive the natural gas that you purchased and pay this transaction price.

The forward price of natural gas depends heavily on *when* it is to be delivered. Prices in winter months are elevated due to the systematically higher demand that we saw earlier in Figure 4.14. Figure 6.2 illustrates an important fact about commodities trading—in almost all circumstances forward prices beyond a few weeks in tenor are traded for delivery over a calendar month. There are distinct forward prices for each month.

Forward curves can move a lot. Figure 6.3 shows a sequence of the NYMEX natural gas forward curves.

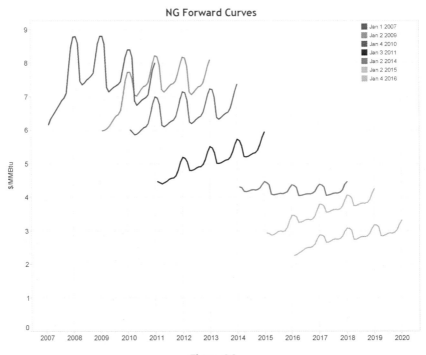

Figure 6.3

Price levels changed dramatically over this period, with the seven forward curves shown spanning a range from under $3/MMBtu to nearly $9/MMBtu. The sustained price drop exhibited by the final three forward curves is a result of shale production. Also, while the shapes of the curves are changing, the dominant differences are shifts in price level—this is what we meant earlier when we stated that change in price level is the primary risk facing the natural longs and shorts.

Backwardation and Contango

Another important observation is that forward curves can be systematically increasing or decreasing with tenor—tenor refers to the time until expiration of the contract. The first curve in Figure 6.3 (Jan 1, 2007) is generally decreasing; the last curve in 2016 is clearly increasing with delivery tenor. There is a particular commodities vernacular to describe this.

When forward prices are decreasing with tenor the curve is said to be *backwardated*; when prices increase with tenor the curve is said to be in *contango*. When forward curves are seasonal, as for natural gas, technically the forward curve is of mixed state—alternating between contango and backwardation. In spite of this seasonal variation, the last few forward curves shown in Figure 6.3 are described as in contango due to the obvious broad trend of increasing price with tenor.

Forward curves become backwardated when supply is running low; conversely, contango tends to occur when there is a surplus. Backwardation incentivizes holders of inventory to release it due to the prevailing near-term premium price. Contango, on the other hand, incentivizes owners of storage facilities to increase inventory, thereby alleviating a supply glut. A storage owner can buy natural gas in the spot market at a low price and store it, simultaneously selling it forward at a higher price for a later delivery month. This earns the storage owner a yield implied by the price differential. We will discuss this concept in more detail in Chapter 7.

Basic Trade Mechanics

Defining a specific trade requires specifying what is being delivered, how much is being delivered and when and where delivery will occur. Timing of delivery and price setting is as important as location. Subtle differences in trade mechanics can cause positions that are seemingly offsetting to become rapidly unbalanced due to minor differences in contracts. We turn now to a few key features that pertain to most natural gas trades.

- Physical versus Financial

Commodities trades are classified according to whether the trade involves physical delivery of the commodity at settlement or merely an exchange of cash flows. The latter type, in which only cash is exchanged between counterparties, are referred to as swaps (you are "swapping" cash flows). Swaps are typically designed to mimic the economics of physical transactions. Although often maligned since the credit crisis (due to what appears to be little more than a phonetic association with credit default swaps), swaps trading broadens the scope of market participants by allowing entities without the extensive infrastructure required to support physical trading to participate nonetheless, ultimately enhancing the depth and liquidity of the markets.

A wide variety of trades exist with arcane and seemingly complex mechanics, but the basic purchase or sale of a commodity is simple. Figure 6.4 shows the flow of natural gas (labelled as MMBtus) and cash for a physical trade. Defining a physical trade amounts to specifying what is going to be delivered; the quantity, time and location of delivery; and, how much will be paid for it.

Basic Trade Diagram

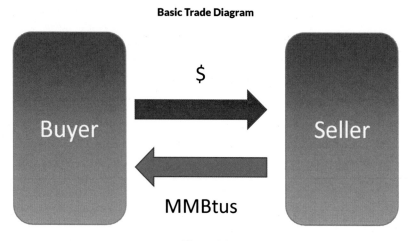

Figure 6.4

A financial trade is different only insofar as cash flows in both directions—the blue MMBtu arrow is replaced by another distinct cash flow. This cash flow is usually designed to be economically similar (ideally nearly identical) to the value of delivery in the physical trade that the swap is intended to mimic. Defining a financial trade involves specifying exactly how much cash flows in each direction.

- Notional

The amount of commodity in a trade is called the *notional* or the *volume* of the trade. This is usually a fixed quantity for a given delivery period[25]. MMBtus (also called dekatherms) are the favored units in the U.S. This is not a global convention. For example, some Canadian trades reference either USD or CAD per gigaJoule (gJ) and large trades can reference metric tons. Trade terms are usually consistent with local or regional volumetric conventions.

A trade confirm in the U.S. will typically specify the notional of a trade in one of the following two forms:

- A specified number of MMBtus for a given delivery period; or:
- A specified number of MMBtus per day or per hour over a given delivery period.

In conversation between traders, notional is usually discussed in units of "lots." A lot is commodities jargon for a standard contract size with the meaning of the term varying by which commodity is being discussed. For natural gas one lot is 10,000 MMBtus. Common vernacular is to refer to the number of lots per delivery day; for example, a "one-a-day" trade for January means one lot per calendar day is to be delivered, implying a total notional of 310,000 MMBtus, which at say $3/MMBtu would be worth $930,000.

---

25 Some esoteric trades involve a variable quantity that is formulaically dependent on temperature indices or actual customer usage. Even in these cases, a notional is defined— after the trade has expired the quantity used to settle the trade is unambiguous.

- Price

Regardless of whether a trade is physical or financial, the price that the buyer of the commodity will pay to the seller must be specified. The most common trades are fixed price trades in which the price is specified at the time of the transaction. For example, the buyer will pay the seller \$3.50/MMBtu.

Financial trades require specification of the cash flows from the seller to the buyer. To understand what it means to sell a commodity financially think about physical trades. Suppose, as above, that you had sold one lot of natural gas to the buyer at \$3.50/MMBtu. This means that at delivery you are obliged to deliver to the buyer 10,000 MMBtus. If you did not have this natural gas you would need to go into the daily (spot) market and procure it at the prevailing price—the spot price. Your economics as a physical trader would be $N\left(p_{fixed} - p_{buy}\right)$ where $N = 10,000$, $p_{fixed} = \$3.50$ and p_{buy} is the price at which you succeeded in buying the natural gas required for delivery.

In a financial trade the seller does not have to purchase the required natural gas at p_{buy} since delivery is never made. Instead, the purchase price is replaced by an index price p_{Index} published by a survey such as Platts Gas Daily. The index used is specified in the trade confirm. If the index is well-designed and the delivery location liquid, insofar as a significant volume of trading is occurring on a daily basis, then it is reasonable to expect the typical physical spot trade to be at a price that is close to the index—in our example, $p_{buy} \approx p_{Index}$. This is the purpose of commodity price indices—a well-designed index results in swaps generating cash flows that are functionally equivalent to a physical transaction.

- Delivery and Settlement

Most natural gas trades reference calendar days or months (also referred to as contract months) as the standard delivery period. A physical trade involves delivery of natural gas *ratably* (uniformly) over the delivery period, unless modifications to this schedule are mutually agreed upon by the buyer and seller. For example, if your trade confirm requires you to deliver 31 lots of natural gas in the month of January, the default delivery schedule is one lot of natural gas per calendar day. There is no embedded optionality in delivery timing for standard natural gas forward contracts. This defines the blue (delivery) arrow in Figure 6.4. The red (payment) arrow is defined by the fixed price p_{fixed}.

Financial trades parallel the mechanics of their physical siblings. For the typical fixed price swap the red (payment) arrow from the buyer to the seller is the same as for a physical transaction. However, the blue delivery arrow now involves the seller paying the buyer the product of the total notional and the average index price over the delivery period. For any particular day d the concept of "delivery" to the buyer is replaced by the seller paying the buyer the economically equivalent amount in cash. The net cash exchanged from the buyer to the seller is: $N\left[p_{fixed} - p_{Index}(d)\right]$. If this amount is negative, the seller pays the buyer.

By the end of a delivery period in a physical contract, the buyer has received the required natural gas but still owes the seller the cash. The trade confirm specifies a date by which such payment, referred to as settlement, is made. Similarly, for a swap the two cash flows (blue and red) are netted and the counterparty owing money to the other must make payment by the specified settlement date.

Hedging Price Risk with Forwards

Hedging refers to any trading activity intended to reduce the risk of an existing position. A company that owns producing natural gas fields is "long" the commodity—it benefits if the price goes up (aside from any hedging activities, which alter the risk profile). Conversely, a consumer of a commodity, as for example a petrochemicals company that requires natural gas as a feedstock, is "short" the commodity, benefitting when the price goes down. Markets exist to allow those with natural long positions to transfer price risk to those who are naturally short, and conversely.

Given how much prices can move (just look back at Figures 6.1 and 6.3), it should come as no surprise that some market participants take measures to reduce price risk. Many consumers of natural gas hedge their future cost by buying it forward using futures or swaps. Similarly, companies which produce natural gas will often sell some amount of expected future production to "lock in" current prevailing forward prices. Company shareholders often expect management to engage in such risk reduction.

- Working Example

On 01Jul2015 your retail natural gas company is short one-a-day at a fixed price p_f = \$3.30 in the month of Oct15. This position should be thought of as what you estimate you will have to deliver to your customers over that month. In the absence of any hedging activity your risk position is as shown in Figure 6.5.

Unhedged Customer Position

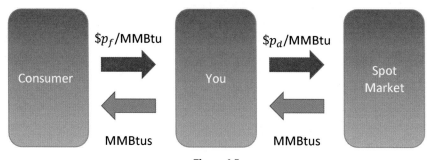

Figure 6.5

Here p_d denotes the daily spot price. This is the price at which you could buy the required natural gas for delivery on day d. Your P&L on this day will be

$10,000 \cdot \left[\$3.30 - p_d \right]$, meaning that you are fully exposed to the uncertainty in the (presently unknown) price p_d.

It is rare (though certainly not unheard of) for a retailer to leave such an exposure unhedged given the obvious risk evidenced in the historical price series. In such a situation it is far more common to hedge—to this end, suppose that on 01Jul2015 you buy one-a-day Henry Hub natural gas for the same delivery month from a counterparty (the seller) at a price of $2.821[26]. We will discuss locational price risk in the next chapter, so for now assume that your customers are located in Louisiana.

The forward purchase requires that your hedge counterparty deliver one lot of natural gas each day for which you will pay the product of the notional quantity and the forward hedge price $F = \$2.821$:

$$310,000 \cdot \$2.821 = \$874,510$$

at a date specified in the trade confirm, usually the first business day preceding the twentieth day of the following month. The result is the situation depicted in Figure 6.6.

Customer Position With Forward Hedge

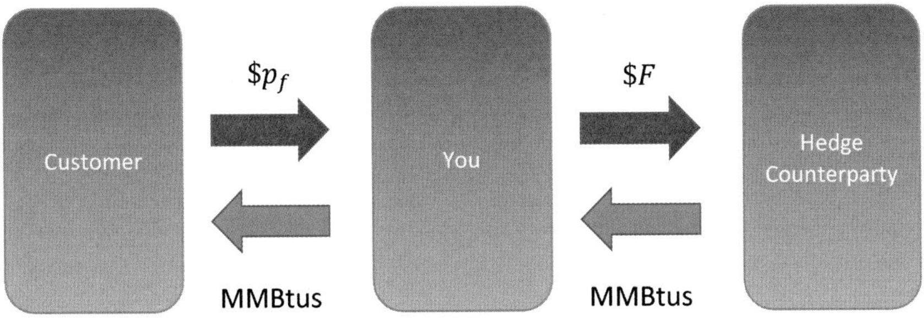

Figure 6.6

The daily payoff is now a fixed and known $10,000 \cdot \left[\$3.30 - \$2.821 \right]$. Commodity price risk has been neutralized.

---

26 It is much more common to contract with customers for longer terms, particularly annual strips, but this example is illustrative.

The Value and Risk of a Forward Trade

Before proceeding with other examples of hedging and trade mechanics, it is important to understand the basic valuation and risk calculations involved in a forward trade.

The present value of any trade is the value that could be achieved by immediately unwinding the trade—that is, doing an offsetting trade to neutralize all price risk[27]. The value of a forward trade changes as forward prices move. For example, by 09Jul2015 the price for Oct15 delivery had decreased to $2.773. This reduced the value of your contract, just as the value of a stock holding drops when the stock prices decreases. The only difference is that to calculate the value of a forward contract (as opposed to a futures contract which we will discuss momentarily), discounting is required.

Continuing with our example, you *could* unwind this trade on 09Jul2015 by selling the same amount of natural gas for Oct15 at the prevailing price. Were you to do so, the result would be a flat position as shown in Figure 6.7 with no net commodity flow. This unwind trade would exactly offset the commodity purchase of the original trade, and at delivery there would remain only a net cash flow.

Unwind of Forward Trade

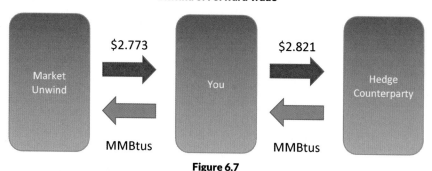

Figure 6.7

Since this cash flow would occur on the settlement date of the Oct15 contract, the value must be discounted to obtain the present value, which gives us:

---

27 Generally the concept excludes such complications as bid/offer spreads and liquidity.

$$V(t) = 0.999 \cdot 310{,}000 \cdot \left[\$2.773 - \$2.821 \right]$$
$$= -\$14{,}865.12$$

which is the product of the notional and the price change *discounted* to the current date[28]. From your perspective the hedge has lost money, or is "out-of-the-money". Your counterparty, who has sold the natural gas to you, is "in-the-money" by the same amount. Note that you as the hedger are not concerned about this since the retail position that you are hedging gained a commensurate value.

More generally, if we denote the forward price prevailing now for delivery at a defined future time by $F_{Current}$ and the initial price at which the original trade occurred by $F_{Initial}$ then the present value of a forward trade for notional N MMBtus is:

$$V = d_{Current} N \left[F_{Current} - F_{Initial} \right]$$

where $d_{Current}$ denotes the current discount factor applicable to the delivery time.

This formula also tells us something about the risk of a forward trade. The delta of a forward contract (the change in value for a small change in the current forward price) is the discounted notional:

$$\Delta = \frac{dV}{dF_{Current}} = d_{Current} N$$

For example, the delta of our Oct15 gas purchase is 309,819 MMBtus, or just under the original 31 lots due to the presence of the discount factor.

If a trading book has forward trades for multiple contract months, then for

---

28 The discount factor (using LIBOR) was 0.999 on this date.

each contract month the book has a delta for the particular forward price. Most risk reports aggregate the deltas of a portfolio in some way that is deemed useful by traders, control groups and management. We will return to this later.

Forward Contracts and Credit Risk

In the example above you purchased 31 lots of natural gas for delivery in Oct15 from your counterparty. This is an example of an over-the-counter (OTC) trade. No other intermediary was involved and by assumption the trade did not occur on a commodity exchange. OTC trades generally result in credit risk.

After only one week the trade above resulted in you owing your counterparty roughly $15K. This is not very much in the greater scheme of things, but the trade was not large and the price change was small. If prices had risen instead, the counterparty would owe you money. On larger trades and in periods of high price volatility, some of your trading counterparties could end up owing you a lot of money. If one of them were to default, in the absence of any collateral posting, you would lose the amount owed. This is credit risk. Compounding matters, you would still be short the natural gas to your customer, meaning you would have to replace the hedge at the current price. This can be expensive, especially if the position is large and you want to replace it quickly to avoid exposure to rapidly changing prices.

Credit risk in OTC trading is usually mitigated by margining, in which the entity with the out-of-the-money (negative PV) positions posts some form of collateral to its trade counterparty, which by definition is in-the-money. OTC trades are almost always transacted between counterparties that have agreements in place which define margining mechanics—ISDAs. Two entities with such documents in place are referred to as "enabled"—they can trade with each other knowing that credit risk will be governed by the terms of these agreements. These documents also specify the remedies should one of the counterparties ever default.

In its simplest form, a margining agreement requires that the total value of the trades between two counterparties be posted by the counterparty who is out of the money. Collateral can be cash, or other guarantees such as letters of credit. More complex margining arrangements can involve thresholds, below which collateral posting is not required and above which it is. In some situations, hedge providers (dealers) structure agreements by which the hedger can use physical assets as collateral. For example, it is not uncommon for owners of electricity generation to use the assets as collateral in support of their hedging activities.

While mitigating credit risk, the enabling process is time consuming and costly. Moreover, it must be done with each counterparty with whom you would like to transact. In short, it can be a barrier to doing business. The purpose of futures exchanges, to which we turn now, is essentially a way to replace the need for multiple counterparties with a single counterparty—the exchange. Moreover, the post credit-crisis regulatory imperative, particularly Dodd-Frank, has had the effect of pushing a large volume of trading activity that was formerly OTC onto exchanges.

Futures Versus Forwards and The Role of Exchanges

Futures exchanges mitigate default exposure by centralizing credit risk. In effect everyone who trades on the exchange is "enabled" with the exchange. The purpose of the exchange is to make sure that each of its counterparties is adequately collateralized, thereby insulating the exchange, and all of the entities that trade through it, from the default of any particular counterparty.

Had you executed your Oct15 hedge on an exchange, it is quite possible that you would have used the NG contract on the New York Mercantile

Exchange (NYMEX), a subsidiary of the CME. This benchmark contract, to which we have already referred repeatedly, was launched in 1990 and is based on physical delivery of natural gas at Henry Hub in Louisiana. Initially only the first 10 contract months traded, which confined liquidity to very short tenors. As of 2017 listed[29] contracts include the current calendar year and the subsequent 12 calendar years.

To illustrate the mechanics of a futures trade we will continue with the same working example, but instead affect the hedge using a purchase of 31 NG Oct15 futures contracts under exactly the same terms.

As with forward contracts, futures trade for delivery in each calendar month. The NYMEX contract has the following basic features:

- One contract has a notional of one lot (10,000 MMBtus).
- Futures contracts expire three business days prior to the start of the delivery month.
- At expiry all holders of long positions are matched with those holding short positions and delivery is arranged between those who are matched.
- Delivery is assumed to be ratable over the contract month unless alternative arrangements are agreed upon between matched counterparties.

By purchasing a futures contract, 31 of them to be precise, you have hedged your price exposure much as you did with the forward purchase. The differences between the two approaches arise in the mechanics of margining and settlement.

- Margining

Upon execution of this trade the exchange requires that you post initial mar-

---

29 The term "listed" means traded on the exchange.

gin, which is held by the exchange in your margin account. The balance in your margin account accrues interest. The amount of initial margin is codified by the exchange and designed to account for netting of risks[30]. Initial margin varies by tenor. As of October 2017 the first three NG contracts require initial margin of \$1980 per contract; at prevailing prices of roughly \$3/MMBtu, this implies a leverage of $\frac{3 \cdot 10,000}{1980} = 15.15$.

On each trading day the exchange posts settlement prices for all contracts. Every trading day all of your futures trades are valued at the settlement price. Any change in the value of your futures trades from the previous settlement is credited to or debited from your margin account. If your margin account balance drops below a threshold, the maintenance margin, then you must post the cash required to bring the margin account balance back to the initial margin level. The purpose of the gap between initial and maintenance margin levels is to prevent large numbers of margin account true-ups for trivial sums. Maintenance margin for the first three contracts stood at \$1800 per contract as of October 2017.

- Settlement

One of the primary activities in which futures exchanges engage is the establishment of daily settlement prices. These are important, not only because of the impact on daily margining calculations, but because they are often used as a basis for daily book valuation for many trading entities. Each exchange has its own protocols for settlement, and in less liquid futures contracts various in-house algorithms are deployed to make what are intended to be reasonable inferences based upon whatever market activity has occurred recently.

Focusing on the NYMEX contract, a common misconception is that set-

---

30 If you are long and short the same commodity in different contracts, margin requirements take this offsetting risk into account. This is easier said than done, and each exchange has its own rules which are often byzantine. For example, CME/NYMEX uses an algorithm called the Standard Portfolio Analysis of Risk (SPAN) which calculates margin requirements for a portfolio of futures positions.

tlement prices are based on trades executed in the last few minutes of each session. This is true for the prompt contract, which is settled using the volumetric weighted average price in the last two minutes of trading, with the exception of the last trading day when the last 30 minutes is used. This is a reliable method as the prompt contract has high volumes of activity throughout the trading day. For longer tenor contracts, lack of liquidity can render this direct form of settlement unworkable, and alternative methods are used. The goal of the exchanges is to use what trading activity exists to post sensible settlement prices for all listed contracts. To this end, the second through sixth nearby contracts are settled using spread trades against the prompt contract. Longer tenors are settled by the exchange using their own algorithms or judgement.

Some trading occurs by direct reference to the daily settlement price. Rather than buying or selling natural gas at whatever prevailing bid or offer exists at a particular moment of the trading session, you can reference the settlement price. Trades of this type are known as "trade-at-settlement" or more commonly as TAS (pronounced "taz"). These can be OTC contracts in which you and a counterparty agree to exchange the commodity at whatever settlement price occurs. On the exchange you simply place your order through your broker. At the end of the session you have a futures position at the settlement price.

Contract Expiration

On the expiration date the contract ceases to trade and, as mentioned above, the longs (buyers) are matched randomly with shorts (sellers), the latter being obliged to deliver the required volumes over the delivery month; the former to pay the final settlement price. Credit risk at this stage is also controlled by the requirement that the buyer post the cash for purchase with exchange clearing members, effectively escrowing the payment. Since many market participants are either not inclined or not technically equipped to take physical delivery of the large volumes of natural gas involved in even a single contract, many futures positions are exited or "closed out" by making offsetting trades prior to expiration.

The Oct15 futures contract expired on 28Sep2015 with a final settlement price of $2.563. Had you taken this position to delivery you would be receiving the natural gas at Henry Hub and paying this price, which is far below your original trade price of $2.821. Note, however that your margin account is negative to the tune of roughly[31] the product of notional and the difference between the trade price and the settlement price, so that in aggregate your original futures trade resulted in the economic equivalent of a purchase of natural gas at the initial trade price of $2.821.

Futures exchanges makes the mechanics of trading easier, especially the initial setup of a new operation, by eliminating the need to become enabled with a host of distinct counterparties. The exchange largely eliminates credit risk via margining. Daily margining does, however, result in slightly different risk attributes of futures compared to forward trades.

Valuation and Risk

At the end of each trading day a futures contract is marked-to-market using settlement prices, and margin accounts are credited or debited accordingly. This means that both the value and the delta of a futures position do not require discounting; the delta is the notional, *not* the discounted notional[32].

The differences in cash-flow mechanics between forwards and futures begs the question: Are forward and futures prices different? The answer is that

---

31 We say roughly since your margin account earns interest.

32 While this last point may seem trivial, sophisticated shops have lost money by forgetting this fact. For example, if you are asked by one of your trading counterparties to clear a forward trade—namely convert an existing OTC forward, in which the PV is the discounted price difference, to a futures exchange, the absence of discounting in the latter can change the value of the new position relative to the original. If the original PV is large and at long tenor where discounting matters, the result can be an unpleasant surprise for one of the counterparties.

they are in general not identical, although in practice the differences are quite small and not worth delving into beyond the following theoretical results:

- If interest rates are constant, forward and futures prices are identical.
- If interest rate changes are uncorrelated with the returns of the commodity, then forwards and futures prices are identical.

The point is that any difference in the two prices is due to correlation between interest rate changes and price returns, and the impact is usually not worth dwelling on[33]. For hedging, aside from the effects of discounting on value and delta, the two types of trades are functionally identical.

Nearby Contracts

Futures contracts have defined expiration dates—for natural gas futures this is three business days before the first day of the delivery month, as mentioned above. This means that every contract has a defined date on which it last trades. There are times, however, when discussion of forward prices requires the concept of "constant maturity". A simple example is calculating the lowest price achieved by the first futures contract over the past year. More advanced questions arise in the context of calculating basic risk metrics, such as how much does a futures price 12 months out move over a ten day time period. Each of these requires using a collection of distinct contract prices.

The simplest way to address such questions is via the concept of nearby contracts. In commodities vernacular the first contract month that is trading

---

33 Correlation between rates and commodities prices is the source of differences between forward and futures prices. For example, in a world in which interest rates tend to increase as commodities prices rise, then the margin account of the holder of a long position in a futures contract is credited when rates are higher, making this position more valuable than for a forward trade. In this case the futures price should be greater than the forward price.

on a particular date is referred to as the first *nearby* contract[34]; the second contract the second nearby and so on. A nearby price series is the concatenation of a set of discrete contract prices, with a given contract rolling off at its expiration date and being replaced with the following contract. Nearby price series, and minor modifications for calculating price returns, are the most common approach to address questions that are inherently constant maturity in nature.

Strips

Up to this point we have discussed forward trades at the level of contract months. In practice, however, individual months are traded liquidly only at short tenors, say within the first twelve calendar months or so. At longer tenors the ergonomics of making markets in individual months becomes cumbersome, and liquidity is concentrated in strips.

A strip is a set of adjacent calendar months, and trading a strip means buying or selling the aggregate of the monthly contracts. Calendar strips, which are comprised of the set of 12 contract months in a calendar year, are the only strips that can be reliably traded at long tenors—by reliably we mean that other strips or individual months would in general have prohibitively high bid/offer spreads. The seasonal nature of demand, and consequently price risk, has also resulted in commonly traded seasonal strips. In summary:

- Calendar strip: A set of 12 contracts corresponding to a calendar year. These are usually referred to as "cal strips", so that "Cal17" refers to the 2017 calendar strip.
- Summer Strip: April through October (the "JV" strip, often phonetically abbreviated by traders as "ape-awk")[35]

---

34 The first contract is also referred to as the "prompt" contract.
35 Contract month abbreviations apply to natural gas as well as to other commodities and some financial instruments such as Eurodollar futures. The twelve calendar months January through December are coded as F, G, H, J, K, M, N, Q, U, V, X, Z. So the Dec17 contract appears on screens as Z17.

- Winter Strip: November through the subsequent March (the 'XH' strip, or phonetically "Novie-March")

The two seasonal strips correspond to the injection and withdrawal seasons.

Figure 6.8 depicts the typical layout of trading screens such as those used when trading on ICE or CME.

Sample Trading Screen

Location	Product	Start Date	End Date	Strip	Qty	Bid	Offer	Qty	Last Trade	Change	Volume	Last Settle
Henry Hub	FP for LD1	1-Dec-17	31-Dec-17	Dec17	5000	3.123	3.129	2500	3.128	-0.006	14,460,000	3.134
					2500	3.121	3.131	5000				
					5000	3.118	3.134	2500				
Henry Hub	FP for LD1	1-Jan-18	31-Jan-18	Jan18	2500	3.212	3.225	5000	3.220	-0.010	7,851,780	3.230
Henry Hub	FP for LD1	1-Feb-18	28-Feb-18	Feb18	5000	3.203	3.238	2500	3.223	-0.015	7,302,155	3.238
Henry Hub	FP for LD1	1-Mar-18	31-Mar-18	Mar18	2500	3.195	3.228	2500	3.211	-0.013	6,791,005	3.224
Henry Hub	FP for LD1	1-Apr-18	30-Apr-18	Apr18	2500	2.940	2.975	5000	2.959	-0.016	6,315,634	2.975
Henry Hub	FP for LD1	1-May-18	31-May-18	May18	5000	2.923	2.956	2500	2.938	-0.017	5,873,540	2.955
Henry Hub	FP for LD1	1-Apr-18	31-Oct-18	Sum18	10000	2.983	2.994	5000	2.990	-0.025	2,447,308	3.015
Henry Hub	FP for LD1	1-Jan-18	31-Dec-18	Cal18	5000	3.052	3.071	5000	3.063	-0.031	2,202,577	3.094

Figure 6.8

There is a lot of information available on a trading screen. In addition to the best bid and offer for each strip, inclusive of volumes available for transaction, the bid/offer stack can be seen, so that the depth of the market and the increase in bid/offer spreads can be ascertained. The last settlement prices and the changes in prices from previous settlements are also shown.

Related Swaps

The NYMEX futures contract as well as OTC forwards involve physical delivery of the commodity for those still holding open positions at the time of contract expiration. Swaps, as we mentioned earlier, involve only transfer of cash. This is an appealing feature for market participants who want to avoid dealing with the hassles of physical delivery, but who have the financial capability to take positions in the markets and in doing so contribute to market liquidity.

A variety of swaps with features very similar to the CME futures contract are traded. Here we will mention only a few that are most commonly encountered.

- *Swaps Which Reference Futures*

Of the many swaps which reference futures contract prices, the most common are the following.

— NYMEX "Look-Alikes"

Sometimes referred to simply as "look-alikes" or "last-day swaps" ("LDs" for short), these swaps settle financially on the price at which the analogous futures contract settled on the day of contract expiration. Settlement from the perspective of a long swap position is:

$$N\left[F_{exp} - K\right]$$

where N denotes the notional (in MMBtus), K the strike of the swap and F_{exp} the settlement price of the futures contract for a specified month on the last trading day of the contract.

In our working example above, the Oct15 expired with a settlement price of $2.563. If, instead of buying natural gas using a futures contract, you had hedged your price exposure using this look-alike swap under the same terms, the settlement amount would have been:

$$310,000 \cdot \left[\$2.563 - \$2.821\right] = -\$79,980$$

The risk of these swaps differs from that of the underlying futures contract in an important way. At expiration of a futures contract, the holder of a long position will take physical delivery of the natural gas in the upcoming month. This means that the delta of the position remains unchanged, and subsequently amortizes off during the delivery month as natural gas is received. The swap, in contrast, ceases to have any price exposure at expiration.

L3D Swaps

"Last three day", or L3D swaps, are designed to reduce the risks associated with settlement on a single trading day by referencing the average of the last three settlement prices of the futures contract prior to and including the expiration date. This design also results in swaps that behave in a fashion similar to bid week price setting, which we will discuss more in Chapter 8. The settlement amount for a long position is:

$$N\left[\overline{F}^{(3)} - K \right]$$

where $\overline{F}^{(3)}$ denotes average of the final three settlement prices. Continuing with our working example, the last three settlement prices of Oct15 averaged to \$2.573 resulting in a settlement value of:

$$310,000 \cdot \left[\$2.573 - \$2.821 \right] = -\$76,880$$

As with the look-alike swaps, the risk profile of L3D swaps differs from futures contracts. In this case, rather than the exposure dropping to zero at expiration as the look-alike does, L3D swaps lose one-third of the initial delta each day during the averaging window.

- Penultimate Swaps

The term penultimate refers to one business day prior to the futures expiration date. Penultimate swaps reference this price, and the settlement amount for a long position is:

$$N\left[\,F_{pen} - K\,\right]$$

The penultimate settlement F_{pen} of the Oct15 contract was \$2.564 yielding a settlement value of:

$$310{,}000 \cdot \left[\,\$2.564 - \$2.821\,\right] = -\$79{,}670$$

An important characteristic of "pen swaps" is that the settlement date coincides with the expiration date of standard listed options. This makes them a favored options hedging instrument. As with look-alikes the price exposure of the penultimate swaps vanishes at the end of the penultimate trading day.

- Comparison

It is tempting to view the differences between these various swaps as insignificant, and at long tenors the differences are not particularly important—the exposures can be aggregated. However, as expiration nears and prices begin to fix, the distinctions in risk behavior can result in rapid changes in risk. A balanced position can quickly become altogether unbalanced when a pen swap expires leaving your portfolio with only futures positions.

Markets have evolved to help manage the risks of trade mismatch. It is straightforward, for example, to "roll" your pen swaps to LD, effectively transforming all residual risks to futures settlement. Nevertheless, many an inexperienced trader (or one on vacation who failed to arrange proper backup) has found themselves unintentionally playing Russian roulette with the brief but large exposures that can arise by failing to pay attention to the expiration mismatches and roll-offs.

The different swap price fixings, while usually quite similar, can occasionally deliver surprises. When price volatility is high in the last few days before contract expiry occurs, the behavior of distinct swaps can become decoupled. One of the more dramatic examples occurred as the Mar2003 contract expired during a period of low inventory and cold temperatures. The price series is shown in Figure 6.9.

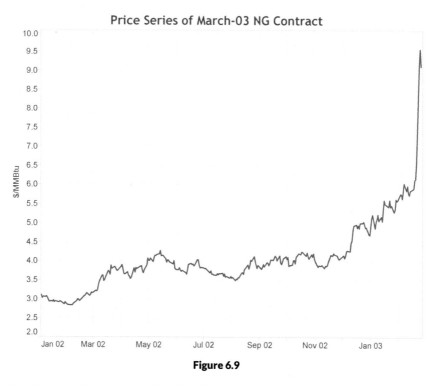

Figure 6.9

In this case the averages for the LD, L3D and Pen swaps were: $9.133, $9.282 and $9.577 respectively. The roughly 5% change in price between penultimate and last-day expiration was quite large, arguably validating the concerns of some market participants regarding settling a swap on a single trading date.

Finally, it is important to keep in mind that using these swaps to hedge price exposure has a very important limitation. In the case of the LD swap, for example, the instant that the futures contract expires, the swap settles financially and there is no obligation for delivery—the delta from the swap vanishes instantaneously. If you had chosen to use a swap in our working example, you would have hedged the price risk from the trade date to contract expiry. However, at expiry you immediately have price risk through the delivery month. This is also true of the penultimate swap shifted one day earlier. In the case of the L3D swap the delta decreases by 1/3 over each of the last three trading days.

Figure 6.10 contrasts the various risk profiles of the futures contract and these related swaps.

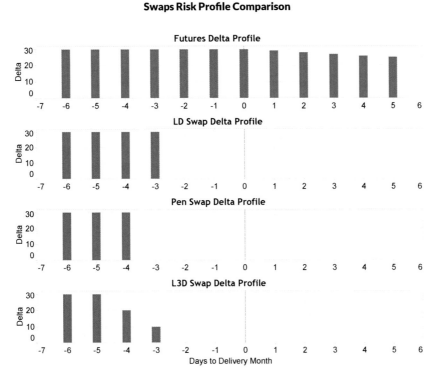

Figure 6.10

Our convention here is that the delivery month starts on day 1; moreover, we have not distinguished between business days and calendar days. The futures delta decreases daily through the delivery month, which is only partially shown.

- Swaps Which Reference Delivery

Here we describe just a few basic swaps used to hedge daily price risk through the delivery month. Later, when we discuss locational price risk in Chapter 8, we will discuss some of these trades in more detail.

- Exchange-for-Swaps

These swaps, also referred to as "EFS", are not swaps per se but are closely related and warrant discussion. An EFS is a mechanism to convert a swap to a futures contract and conversely. Suppose in our working example that you were using the LD look-alike swap to hedge a daily physical position in Oct15. In the absence of any action on your part, when the swap settles at expiration you no longer have any hedge in place for your short gas position. However, before expiry you can buy an EFS, paying (or in rare cases receiving) a small spread, usually a fraction of a cent. This transaction is immediately reported to the exchange, at which point your swap is replaced with a bona fide futures contract. At expiry the futures position results in physical delivery, which is what you need to hedge your short position through the month.

Gas Daily Swing Swaps

These are swaps that settle on the gas daily index published by Platts. While there are other services that provide price surveys, Platts Gas Daily Average (GDA or GD for short) is the index most often used for daily swaps. For each day d in a delivery month the swap settles on the difference between the gas daily index price $p_{GD}(d)$ and the fixed strike K of your swap:

$$N\left[p_{GD}(d) - K\right]$$

As usual N is the notional. The final settlement is the sum of these values over all days in the month.

As an example, suppose that you agree to sell natural gas to a customer at a price of $2.80/MMBtu knowing that you can hedge this position by buying a GDA swap at a price of $2.60/MMBtu. This situation is depicted in Figure 6.11;

Customer Position Hedge With GD Swap

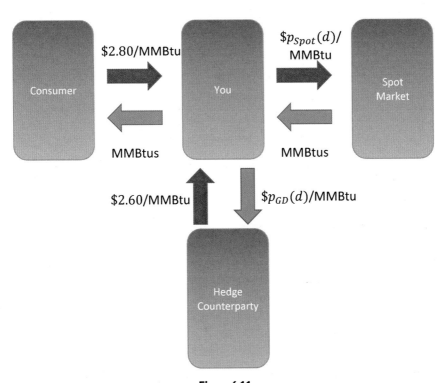

Figure 6.11

The result is that you have $0.20/MMBtu of margin and a residual risk position of $p_{GD} - p_{spot}$:

- $p_{GD}(d)$ is what you receive from your swap;
- $p_{spot}(d)$ is what you have to pay to actually acquire the natural gas in the daily market.

If the GD price is "close" to the actual spot price, which is what a well-designed index is supposed to accomplish, then you are hedged and have effectively locked in your $.20/MMBtu of profit. Note also that the price risk of a GD swap amortizes linearly to zero over the delivery month, just as ratable physical delivery does.

A gap exists between the gas daily swing swaps and the NG futures contract and its related swaps. The former have payoffs that are a function of daily spot prices; the latter expire prior to a delivery month at a single fixed price. The price exposure of gas daily swing swaps amortize over the delivery month; that of the futures-based swaps vanish before the delivery month. There is a set of trades that span these gaps, notably basis and index futures. Since these trade types are designed to "move risk" from NG futures with delivery at Henry Hub to *different* delivery locations, we defer discussion to Chapter 8 where we discuss basis trading.

Index Integrity

The last two examples illustrate a very important point about the use of financial hedges against physical positions: *for the hedge to work, the index must provide an accurate representation of transactions in the physical market.*

The importance of this point cannot be overstated. So far, we have assumed that all of the risks and hedging activities are occurring at Henry Hub, which is an unambiguously liquid delivery location. At less liquid delivery locations, a situation discussed more in Chapter 8, a price index is less reliable since supporting trade data is provided by only a small number of market participants. This can result in swaps hedges being less effective than the hedger was expecting.

In the aftermath of the credit crisis, the ensuing enthusiasm of regulators to "crack down" on index manipulation has resulted in many long-standing and well-behaved market participants ("good citizens" so to speak) ceasing to submit their physical trade data to index providers like Platts or NGI. There is little to be gained from submission of trade data, aside from a general notion that if submissions stop altogether then markets will cease to function efficiently. Now, however, the prospect of large fines (or worse) should trading activity be deemed inappropriate by the likes of the CFTC or the FERC serves to diminish market transparency rather than enhance it. As a result, many indices are now less reliable, and arguably even easier for those remaining participants to distort the markets should they be so inclined.

CHAPTER 7

Time Spreads

FORWARD CURVES ARE dynamic, evolving continuously throughout each trading day. Changes in a forward curve are usually dominated by shifts in price levels—all forward prices moving in tandem up or down. This empirical fact is true for all energy forward curves, including natural gas, and explains why hedging protocols typically start with efforts to control exposure to absolute price level.

The second most important statistical feature of price dynamics relates to the spread between prices at short delivery tenors and those at longer tenors—so called time spreads. Although these are much less likely to appear in the typical news wire or financial publication, time spreads are an essential component of the activities of most trading desks.

A time spread is simply a position in which you are long one contract month or strip, and short another with a different delivery time, both at the same delivery location. For example, a long position in a Henry Hub Apr-Oct17 (phonetically "Ape-Awk") spread, means that you are long the Apr17 contract and short the same amount of the Oct17 contract. Each position, the long and short, are sometimes referred to as "legs" of the spread.

When discussing time spreads, the default assumption is that the long and short legs are of the same (or nearly the same) notional. Trade mechanics can result in the notional position of the long and short legs being slightly different. If, for example, you buy one-a-day of Mar17 and sell one-a-day of

Apr17, then you are long one extra lot simply due to the fact that March has one more calendar day than does April.

A time spread can be created by buying one contract and, in a separate transaction, selling the other; but this is not how it is usually done. Time spreads are so commonly traded that they are priced and appear on trading screens as a package. This reduces the risk of slippage that could occur due to timing differences in comparison to executing each leg separately. It also lowers bid/offer spreads since you are not paying the offer and receiving the bid on distinct trades.

There are two primary reasons that time spreads are important. The first is that they provide a direct mechanism for creating exposure to the level of backwardation or contango of the forward curve. As we will see, time spreads respond to inventory level much as outright positions move in response to changes in supply and demand. The second, and more important reason, is that liquidity is heavily concentrated in short tenor contracts. If you need to quickly hedge a long tenor price exposure, you will buy or sell short tenor contracts and then later move these hedges to longer tenors using time spreads. This hedging protocol is referred to as "stack-and-roll". We will discuss both of these concepts in more detail in what follows.

Trading Time Spreads

Time spreads are usually quoted as the difference between the price of the shorter tenor position and that of the longer tenor position[36]. The spread is positive when the forward curve is backwardated, and negative when it is contango. This means that buying a spread is taking a long position in the near-dated contract or strip, and a short position of roughly equal notional

---

36 This convention, unfortunately, is not universal. The protocol on NYMEX is that buying the spread involves the purchase of the premium contract; that is, whichever contract is more expensive. In this case all spreads are positive, and you have to know which contract is premium. Why this somewhat ridiculous convention lives on is a mystery.

in the longer tenor leg. Figure 7.1 depicts a trading screen layout for time spreads—this is a stylized representation of platforms such as ICE.

Sample Time Spread Trading Screen

Location	Product	Tenor	Qty (MMBtu)	Bid	Offer	Qty (MMBtu)	Last Trade	Change	Volume	Last Settle
Henry Hub	NG LD1 Futures Spread	Jan18/Apr18	2500	0.320	0.323	2500	0.319	-0.003	325,000	0.322
			5000	0.319	0.324	5000				
			5000	0.317	0.325	2500				
Henry Hub	NG LD1 Futures Spread	Jan18/Feb18	2500	-0.001	0.002	5000	0.001	0.002	145,000	-0.001
Henry Hub	NG LD1 Futures Spread	Mar18/Apr18	2500	0.280	0.303	2500	0.302	-0.015	162,500	0.317
Henry Hub	NG LD1 Futures Spread	Apr18/May18	5000	0.027	0.031	2500	0.029	-0.002	55,000	0.031
Henry Hub	NG LD1 Futures Spread	May18/Jun18	2500	-0.025	-0.021	5000	-0.020	-0.002	90,000	-0.018

Figure 7.1

The first (best) bid of $.320 on Jan18/Apr18 spread shown in the figures means that someone is willing to pay this spread per unit notional to enter a long position. The size of this bid is shown as 2500 MMBtus/day for each of the legs. Should you wish to sell this spread (enter a short Jan18 and long Apr18 position) you could transact up to 2500/day, receiving $0.320/ MMBtu; if you wanted to sell an additional 5000/day you could do this at the level of the second bid of $0.319. The best offer of $0.323 is the price at which you could buy 2500 MMBtus of this spread—you would then have a long Jan18, short Apr18 spread.

Stack-and-Roll Hedging

Liquidity tends to decrease as the tenor of the trade increases. This is a common feature across asset classes—as tenor increases there are fewer active hedgers and speculators have a harder time forecasting payoffs. Some markets, however, support trading on comparatively long time scales. A 30 year USD LIBOR swap, for example, is relatively straightforward to trade. In energy, however, the situation is more precarious. Crude oil benchmarks such as Brent and WTI can be readily traded out to roughly ten years in tenor. For natural gas, although the Henry Hub NG contract is listed on the exchange for 12 years, liquidity diminishes rapidly after roughly five years in tenor. For closely related electricity markets, liquidity becomes a concern after only a few years at even the most liquid locations.

The drop in liquidity with tenor can be seen directly from exchange data. Figure 7.2 shows the average daily trading volume and open interest (the number of outstanding contracts) for first 24 NG nearby futures contracts from 2010 to 2015.

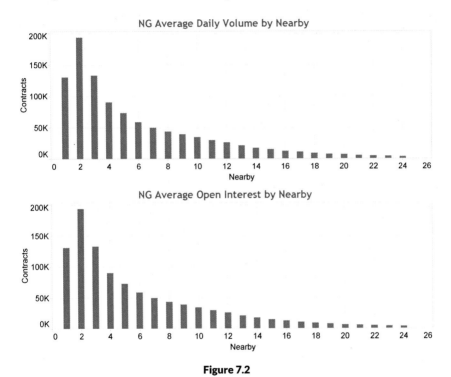

Figure 7.2

The higher open interest in the second nearby contract is due to the fact that financial participants roll their positions from the first to second nearby well before expiry. The most important feature, however, is the rapid decay in liquidity at longer tenors. When you are trying to hedge long dated risk, it is simply harder to trade the volumes required.

This drop in liquidity poses challenges. In situations like the working example in Chapter 6, where the risk being hedged involves modest volumes within the first few calendar years, hedging is a routine affair. However, situations frequently arise in which risk extends over much longer time horizons. Financing the construction of pipelines, storage or natural gas-fired generation requires loans with maturity spanning the better part of a decade, and lenders require hedges for the term of the loans. Municipalities will also occasionally purchase several decades of their forecasted natural gas requirements, incentivized by tax benefits for doing so. As transaction volumes and tenors increase, the simple approach of directly hedging your risks becomes untenable due to high transaction costs.

When traders need to hedge long term risk, they often implement a "stack-and-roll" hedging programs. The train of thought is to initially create an offsetting position as shorter tenors where liquidity is concentrated—this is the "stack" part of the hedge. Subsequently, as circumstances allow, these short tenor hedge positions are "rolled" to longer tenors. Rolling a hedge is nothing more than buying or selling a time spread.

For example, suppose a counterparty approaches you on 01Apr2016 with a request to sell 4 lots/day (in what follows we will say, for example, 4/day for brevity when we mean 4 lots per day) at Henry Hub for Cal17-Cal22. You know that if you do this trade it is unlikely that you will be able to off-load the risk quickly; at least without paying a large bid/offer spread. Nonetheless, you would like the business and want to price the transaction sensibly. Going out to the markets to solicit bids for such a position after the client request is tantamount to acting as a broker, which often spooks the market and annoys the client. This situation requires a stack-and-roll hedging program, and the transaction should be valued accordingly.

You know that you could quickly sell Cal17 swaps to balance the position. Figure 7.3 shows the delta by contract month of the initial trade in green. A stacked hedge of -13.75/day of Cal17 is shown in blue, and the net risk position once this stack hedge is in place appears in orange.

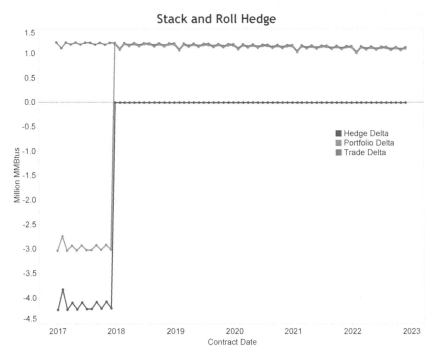

Figure 7.3

The small monthly variations in volume are due to day count. We will discuss how we arrived at the Cal17 hedge volume momentarily; the method used is statistical in nature and somewhat technical[37].

The stack hedge is intended to neutralize the portfolio to macroscopic shifts in the price level across the curve, the near term short position offsetting the long tenor position. Your portfolio remains exposed to changes in backwardation/contango—if the forward curve flattens (less contango) you will lose money. Nonetheless, this stacked position is much less risky than the original unhedged position since the dominant risk of price level changes has been neutralized.

Why did we choose to sell -13.75/day of Cal17? The total delta of the original trade was in fact 8406 lots, and the delta of our hedge merely -4971 lots.

---

37 While we prefer the statistical methodology, in practice it is more common for a trader to decide on the stack volume as a matter of "judgement".

The reason is that price volatility decreases with tenor. Figure 7.4 shows the historical returns volatility for the natural gas forward curve by tenor calculated using market data from 2012-2015.

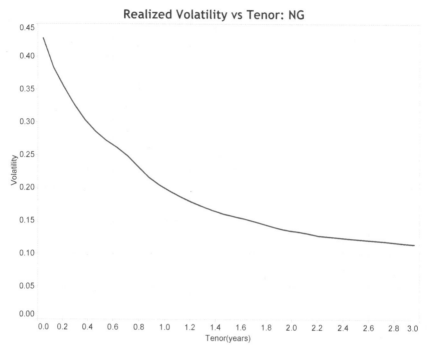

Figure 7.4

This figure shows a very important statistical feature of forward price dynamics—longer tenor contracts tend to move less than nearer dated contracts.

An immediate consequence of the drop in volatility with tenor is that a smaller delta at a shorter tenor is "equivalent" to a larger delta at a longer tenor—the shorter tenor price will (at least statistically speaking) move more. You need to hold less notional at short tenors to mitigate the price volatility at longer tenors. The hedge quantity used in this example was obtained by minimizing the variance of the total portfolio. The details of how this was done are provided at the end of this chapter in Insert 7.1.

Once this "stacked" hedge is in place, the typical course of action is to look for opportunities to efficiently roll the hedge forward, for example selling Cal18 or beyond and buying back some fraction of the original Cal17 hedge. The goal is to keep the position neutral to price level changes along the way. The roll is most efficiently accomplished by trading time spreads; in this case the Cal17/ Cal18 calendar spreads. Time spreads are an efficient way to "move delta out the curve", and are so central to this activity that they are in fact commonly referred to as "rolls" by traders ("Where is the 17/18 roll trading?").

Eventually the original trade is reduced to an effectively flat position. The time and cost of affecting the entire stack-and-roll hedge depends on liquidity in the markets over the course of the effort—a cost that is hard to estimate in advance. Less liquidity in the markets at the time of the transaction implies either a greater cost to roll or a longer time in which time spread risk has to be held. It is possible to apply quantitative methods to this topic, but the results are usually over-engineered and predicated on assumptions that are hard to justify; in practice pricing depends on basic heuristics or trader judgement.

Inventory and the Cost of Carry

Inventory levels affect time spreads. To see this it is best to view the forward curve as a yield (interest rate) curve. If you think of the first nearby price as the price at which you can invest money by purchasing natural gas (or any storable commodity for that matter) for near term delivery, the forward prices at longer tenors imply a yield were you to simultaneously sell the commodity forward at longer dates.

We will assume for simplicity that every contract month spans exactly one twelfth of a year, and to keep notation simple we will quote interest rates as monthly rates. If you can buy natural gas for the first nearby at price F_1 and simultaneously sell it forward for delivery in the nth contract month at price F_n, then the yield achieved satisfies:

$$F_n = F_1 \left(1 + y\right)^n$$

This is simply saying that if you borrow F_1 and use it to purchase natural gas for the upcoming delivery month, simultaneously selling the same quantity for n^{th} nearby contract, you will receive a monthly yield y. If the curve is in contango, so that $F_n > F_1$, then this yield is positive; if the curve is backwardated, with $F_n < F_1$, then it is negative. For example, on 07/05/2017, the Aug17 NG contract settled at \$2.840 and the Jan18 at \$3.181. With a five month difference in the delivery tenors the forward yield is 2.294% on a monthly basis.

This forward yield y is a "gross" yield—it is not adjusted for your costs to borrow. It is also not adjusted for the cost you would incur to own or rent the facilities required to store the natural gas between when you take delivery in the first month and deliver it in the later month. To take these costs into account, assume that r is your monthly financing rate for the borrowing, and for simplicity assume that storage costs are expressed as a monthly rate q on the value of the gas stored. The economic incentive to store becomes: y-r-q. You should store the natural gas if the yield y implied by the forward curve is above your total carrying cost of r+q.

Because owners of storage are acutely aware of all of this, forward yields and inventory levels interact—this is what makes consumption commodities particularly interesting. If there is a surplus of natural gas and inventory levels rise, available storage capacity becomes scarce and the forward curve becomes contango. This incentivizes storage owners to absorb the surplus gas by putting it in storage. Conversely, if natural gas is in short supply, near term prices rise, the curve becomes backwardated and yields go negative. Negative forward yields incentivize those with natural gas in storage to withdraw it and sell it, saving themselves from negative carry and simultaneously alleviating the shortage.

This interaction can be viewed in two ways. Figure 7.5 shows the natural gas forward curve on 15Jan2016 in the top plot. The lower plot shows the monthly forward yields—the yields between month n and $n+1$[38]. The forward yields are positive through much of the year, notably during the months where natural gas demand is lowest, and negative during the winter when demand is high, incentivizing storage owners to withdraw. Given that these are *forward* yields, a more accurate statement is that storage owners are *planning* to withdraw in the negative forward yield months, and that they are hedging accordingly.

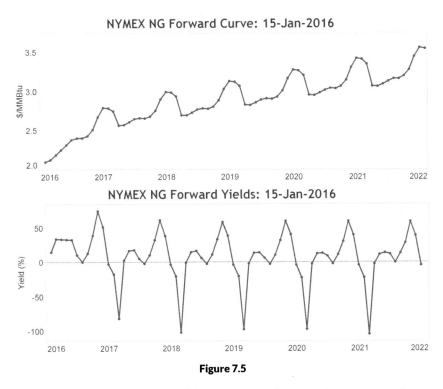

Figure 7.5

Another more dynamic view of the interaction between inventory and storage is shown in Figure 7.6. This is a plot of historical forward yields between the first and second calendar strip prices versus the storage residuals shown in Figure 4.16 from 2000 to 2015. Calendar strips are used to reduce distortions due to seasonality.

---

38 These are continuous time yields y_n between months n and n+1 satisfying: $F_{n+1} = F_n e^{\frac{y_n}{12}}$, or equivalently $y_n = 12\log\left[\frac{F_{n+1}}{F_n}\right]$.

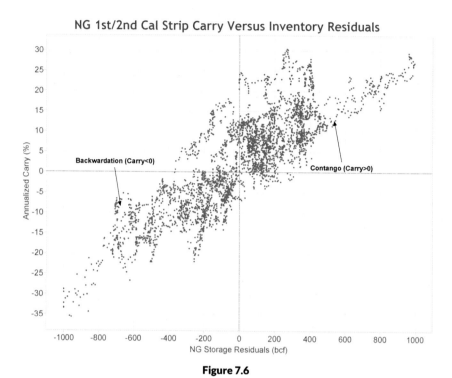

Figure 7.6

At high levels of inventory the forward curve is biased toward contango—higher forward yields are required to incentivize storage operators to hold high levels of inventory. Another way of looking at it is that the relatively smaller amount of available storage capacity makes it worth more.

Finally a cautionary statement is in order. Forward yields are the dominant signal to storage owners. However, as we saw earlier, physical storage has constraints on how fast you can inject or withdraw. When the cost of carry goes negative, storage owners cannot sell their entire inventory instantly. These physical constraints make the calculations involved in rigorous optimization of storage extremely challenging. The behavior of storage operators is, therefore, hard to predict with any degree of precision. On long time scales, however, the theme is clear: inventory and forward yields are closely related.

Park and Loans

We turn next to park-and-loans, which are a class of physical transactions often used to exploit the differences in borrowing rates between storage owners and higher rated lenders. This commonly traded structure is best understood in terms of forward yields.

The term park-and-loan is actually a concatenation of two separate transactions. First, "park" (or "parking") refers to delivering natural gas to a pipeline/storage operator with an agreement to take it back at a specified time in the future—for a fee. Conversely a "loan" refers to withdrawing natural gas from the system now, agreeing to return an equivalent amount at a specified future time. In daily operations parking and loaning is routinely done over short time scales to balance short term fluctuations in physical trading operations[39]. However, longer term transactions spanning injection and withdrawal seasons are common.

Consider the situation of an owner of storage capacity who, on trade date 01Apr2016, is considering injecting during Jul16 and withdrawing an identical volume the following January (Jan17). Available storage capacity endows the owner with a short spread position—remember, a long time spread position means being long the shorter tenor contract and short the longer tenor. The value of storage in this case increases as the Jul16 contract price falls (it is cheaper to procure the gas for storage) and increases as the Jan17 contract price rises (the inventory can be sold at a higher price). If the storage owner wants to lock in the current spread implied by the forward curve, then natural gas must be purchased for Jul16 and sold for Jan17.

Assuming that the storage facility is at or near Henry Hub, the prevailing forward prices on 01Apr2016 were $2.155 for Jul16 and $2.863 for Jan17. The implied annual yield over this period is 56.35%[40]. Upon expiration of the Jul16

39 For readers with a rates background this is analogous to overnight repos.
40 Here again, while any standard rate convention works just fine, we are using continuous time rates, with the yield being $\frac{1}{0.504}\log\left[\frac{\$2.863}{\$2.155}\right]$ where 0.504 is the time in fractions of a year between the two contracts.

149

contract the owner must pay cash for the delivered commodity; cash that is borrowed at the funding rate of the storage operator. Supposing that this rate for the period in question is 8.00%, the effective return for the operator is 48.35%.

Pipeline companies and storage operators, however, are not typically strong credits—often they are barely investment grade. This means that their cost to fund the inventory purchase is greater than it would be for higher rated entities such as banks with strong credit ratings. It is this disparity in borrowing rates that creates a natural funding arbitrage—the storage operator is set up to deal with the physical aspects of managing and operating its facilities; however the stronger credit bank has the funding advantage.

The natural outcome is a park-and-loan transaction in which the bank agrees to purchase the natural gas for the injection month and to take delivery during the withdrawal month. Assuming, for example, that the funding rate for the bank is 2% this increases the effective return by 6.00%. This difference can have a significant economic impact; on a transaction size of say 1bcf at the Jul16 price of $2.155 the result is an economic gain of $66,177.

The owner of the storage facility does not give the storage capacity to the bank for free. The bank pays the operator for the capacity in some fashion—either as an upfront payment or as payments split in some fashion over the course of the transaction. Another way of saying this is that the operator and the bank split the financing gain of 6.00%. The owner then obtains some excess return, say 1% over the original 48.35%; and the bank, acting effectively as a lender, makes the rest.

Time Spread Risk: Bull and Bear Spreads

Time spreads can also be used to reflect a trading view (speculate) on whether the forward curve will steepen (increasing forward yields and more backwardation) or flatten. This is usually done by buying or selling the time spread.

Time spreads, however, are not neutral from a price level risk perspective.

A single time spread has equal notional on each leg. As we saw earlier, forward prices at longer tenors are typically less volatile than those at shorter tenors. This means that time spreads are fundamentally unbalanced from the perspective of price level risk. Figure 7.7 shows the realized values for the Cal16 and Cal17 strips, and a scatter plot of the Cal16/Cal17 calendar spread versus the underlying Cal16 strip price.

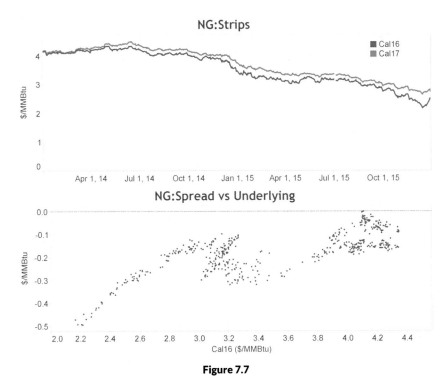

Figure 7.7

The top plot shows the more rapid drop in the Cal16 price versus Cal17 as prices decreased. The lower plot shows the spread versus the underlying price level. The embedded long position in the spread is clearly visible. If you have a single time spread, you are also usually long or short to some degree.

Spreads that are inherently long are referred to as "bull spreads" and those that are short are called "bear spreads". This vernacular is merely acknowledging what is well known by traders—each spread has a typical response to the underlying price level. In Insert 7.2 at the end of the chapter, we discuss spread dynamics in more detail, relating the embedded risk to the price levels and relative volatilities of the two legs. As a general rule, however, a long spread position (long the near dated contract) is a bull spread. In market dialog the terms bull spread and bear spread are used synonymously with long and short spreads respectively.

Seasonal Spreads

Most of our examples above involved time spreads with contract months separated by one year. This made statistical analysis easier by reducing the potential effects of seasonality. Spreads between different calendar months trade routinely, especially at shorter tenors. Recall Figure 7.5, which showed month-on-month implied yields (annualized) exceeding 50% in contango and -100% in backwardation. These large and volatile yields spawn a great deal of market activity.

The most interesting seasonal spreads are those that span the boundaries of the injection and withdrawal seasons. These spreads are viewed as capturing the essential features of season-to-season storage considerations. They also tend to exhibit relatively high levels of volatility and are challenging to model.

Figure 7.8 shows the historical behavior of the Oct/Jan spreads and forward yields for 2009 and 2015. The background shows the bounds of these spreads and yields for the ten years spanning 2006 to 2015. The data used for each series started one year before October—the x-axis is indexed in days prior to 01Oct, with say -350 being 350 days before the delivery month.

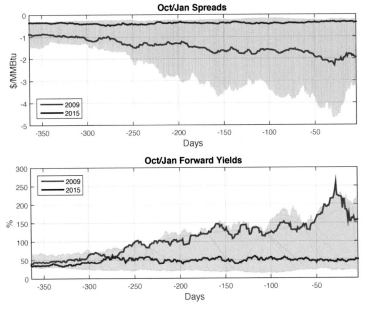

Figure 7.8

The two highlighted years illustrate the challenges in modeling seasonal spreads. In 2015 the forward yields between Oct and Jan were relatively stable near 50%. In contrast 2009 showed yields approaching 250%. Yet, as shown in Figure 7.9, the inventory trajectories over these years were quite similar.

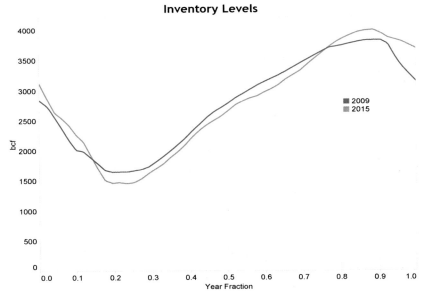

Figure 7.9

The extreme behavior of the 2009 trajectory was primarily the result of credit-crisis turbulence. While inventory is an important driver of seasonal spreads, it is by no means the only relevant factor.

The other dominant seasonal spread is Mar-Apr. Figure 7.10 shows this spread with 2006 (pre-shale gas) and 2015 (post-shale gas) highlighted. Once again, the background represents the envelope of values achieved for the Mar-Apr spread from 2006 to 2015.

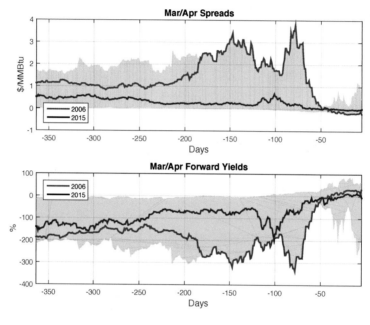

Figure 7.10

Prior to the credit crisis and the near contemporaneous onslaught of shale gas, the Mar-Apr spread frequently exhibited very high volatility, earning it the name "the widow-maker" among traders. Shale gas production, however, has resulted in a taming of the spread; it is currently of much less interest than before, trading at or near parity most of the time. However, from a forward yield perspective, even recent behavior remains interesting.

The moral of the story for each of these particular spreads is that while common themes are discernible, such as the general effects of price level and inventory, additional drivers can sporadically (and at times unpredictably) drive spread behavior in a fashion that is at variance with common folklore or statistical expectation.

Insert 7.1: Stack-And-Roll Hedge Calculations

Constructing a minimum variance hedge of a position with current value V using a hedge with value H involves finding the hedge weight α which minimizes the total portfolio variance:

$$Var\left[\Delta V - \alpha \Delta H\right]$$

Here ΔV and ΔH are the change in values over some time period, for example a single trading day. The solution is:

$$\alpha = \frac{\sigma_V \rho_{VH}}{\sigma_H} \qquad (7.1)$$

where σ_V and σ_H are the standard deviations of the change in values ΔV and ΔH respectively, and ρ_{VH} is the correlation between them. The result makes sense—if two assets are perfectly correlated, the optimal hedge is simply the ratio of the volatilities.

Now suppose you are trying to hedge a notional N of futures contract with price F_1 using another contract with price F_2. The returns of the first price are $\frac{\Delta F_1}{F_1}$, similarly for the second contract. Using (7.1) yields:

$$\alpha = N \frac{\sigma_1 F_1 \rho}{\sigma_2 F_2}$$

where σ_1 and σ_2 are the respective returns volatilities, and ρ is the correlation between the two returns.

When dealing with strips of contract prices, each strip value is defined by weights. For example, if the original trade strip is defined by a vector of monthly weights $\overline{W}$ equal to the notional in each month, and that of the hedge strip by $\overline{w}$, then we have:

$$\alpha = \frac{\left(\overline{wF}\right)^t A\left(\overline{WF}\right)}{\left(\overline{wF}\right)^t A\left(\overline{wF}\right)}$$

where A is the covariance matrix of returns.

In calculating the optimal stack hedge earlier in this chapter the returns covariance was calculated using data from 2012-2015.

Insert 7.2: Time Spread Risk Decomposition

A more formal way to look at spread dynamics is to break the vanilla spread into a balanced position and a residual position. Consider a long spread position; the change in value over a period of time is:

$$\Delta V_{spread}\left(t\right) = \Delta F_1\left(t\right) - \Delta F_2\left(t\right) \qquad (7.2)$$

where $F_1\left(t\right)$ and $F_2\left(t\right)$ denote the forward prices for delivery at $T_1 < T_2$ respectively. Recalling our analysis of the "roll" in the previous section, in particular (7.1) in Insert 7.1, the balanced minimum-variance position for one T_2 contract involves holding:

$$\alpha = \rho_{12}\left(\frac{\sigma_2}{\sigma_1}\right)\left(\frac{F_2}{F_1}\right)$$

of the T_1 contract. Here the subscripts 1 and 2 again refer to the respective legs. This means that:

$$\Delta F_2(t) = \alpha \Delta F_1(t) + \varepsilon(t)$$

where ε is a residual that is uncorrelated with price changes.

If we use this in (7.2) we have:

$$\Delta V_{spread}(t) = \left[1 - \alpha\right]\Delta F_1(t) + \varepsilon(t)$$

The implication is that if $\alpha < 1$ we are dealing with a bull spread since the value of the spread increases (statistically) as the value of the underlying commodity price F_1.

Correlation is bounded by unity $\rho_{12} \leq 1$, and backwardation of volatility means that typically $\frac{\sigma_2}{\sigma_1} < 1$. Therefore, as long as the price ratio $\frac{F_2}{F_1}$ is not too large, the result is that $\alpha < 1$ and that a long spread is in fact a bull spread. In summary, backwardation of volatility is the reason that long spreads are usually bear spreads.

CHAPTER 8

Basis Markets

THE VALUE OF most commodities varies by location. Prices are generally lower where production occurs and higher at places where demand is located. This is certainly true for natural gas, which requires a substantial infrastructure to move it from where it is produced to where it is needed. High demand in a particular region can result in high prices, incentivizing those who can transport natural gas from other lower priced regions to do so. Price differentials pay for transport infrastructure.

If you are considering building a natural gas-fired power plant, you need to know the cost to procure gas at the precise location of the asset. Likewise, if you are acquiring a portfolio of natural gas consumers, you need to know where they are, how they behave and the cost of getting natural gas to them when they need it. The cost of transport is a primary driver of price differentials; locational price risk arises from changes in the amount of available transport capacity relative to demand for its use.

In energy markets *basis* is the difference between the price at a particular geographical delivery point and a benchmark price. In U.S. natural gas markets the common understanding is that basis refers to the price differential between a delivery location and Henry Hub, Louisiana, the delivery location of the benchmark NG futures contract. Although basis is technically a spread, people use the phrase *basis trading* as a general term for the trading of natural gas at delivery locations other than Henry Hub. Basis desks commonly engage in a variety of trades that make no reference to Henry Hub futures—we will discuss some of these shortly. However, regardless of the exact nature of their activities, almost all basis desks make use of the benchmark futures contract, and most view their risks in reference to it.

Many factors affect the relationships between locational prices and Henry Hub. Fluctuations in weather can cause rapid variation in regional demand and, therefore, price. Technological innovations can alter the geographical distribution of production, and over longer time scales change basis dynamics. Finally, when parts of the physical system fail, such as a pipeline suffering a sudden loss in capacity, large and unpredictable changes in locational prices can occur. All of these factors contribute to basis risk.

The first step in managing locational price risk is to understand what is actually involved in the physical delivery of natural gas to end users. This requires some basic knowledge about the pipeline system and how it works.

Pipelines and Delivery

Pipelines are to basis risk as storage is to time spreads. The pipeline system facilitates (and constrains) the movement of natural gas from producing fields and storage facilities to end-users. Whether you are developing a producing field or a natural gas-fired generator, a primary consideration in any investment is where you can connect to the pipeline system, how much it will cost you to do so, and how reliable the delivery will be.

The U.S. interstate pipeline network was shown in Figure 5.2. The purpose of this figure was purely to illustrate the extent of the system, and is of very little practical use. Maps are, however, an integral part of a physical natural gas desk's activities and are often provided by the pipeline companies. Such maps, which identify the delivery points along a pipeline, are almost overwhelmingly detailed—this should come as no surprise given that the system is capable of receiving and delivering natural gas to customers scattered across the country.

- The Pipeline Companies

The first organizing principle in natural gas transport is the individual pipeline company. Figure 8.1 shows the Texas Eastern Transmission (TETCO) pipeline system. The TETCO system, to which we have already made frequent reference, is an interstate pipeline that spans the eastern U.S., connecting the Southeast and Gulf regions to the New York City area. There are many pipeline companies in the country; we are using TETCO purely as a representative (and important) example. If you use the TETCO system to supply natural gas to your customers in New Jersey, you contract directly with TETCO. As with all interstate pipelines, a tariff system is in place that defines types and costs of transport, and the operational procedures on the pipeline.

- Zones

The value of natural gas depends on where it is delivered along a pipeline. A pipeline system is partitioned into distinct delivery areas called zones[41]. The zone is the second organizing principle. Figure 8.1 also shows the delivery zones overlaid on the TETCO system.

---

41 The use of the word "zone" to denote such partitions is not universal. TETCO, for example, uses the term "Market Area"

TETCO Zones

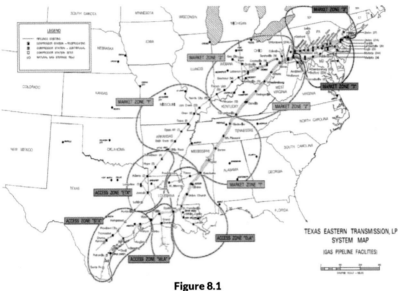

Figure 8.1

Tariffs define the cost of transport as a function of the zone in which the gas is injected into the pipeline and the zone in which it is withdrawn. Figure 8.2 shows the variable (usage) cost between zones in $/MMBtu.

TETCO Variable Transport Rates

Pursuant to sections 3.2 (A) and 3.3 (A) of Rate Schedule FT-1:

Usage-1 - Maximum	STX	WLA	ELA	ETX	M1	M2	M3
from STX	0.0047	0.0052	0.0096	0.0096	0.0240	0.0503	0.0677
from WLA	0.0052	0.0027	0.0064	0.0064	0.0208	0.4710	0.0645
from ELA	0.0096	0.0064	0.0046	0.0046	0.0190	0.0453	0.0627
from ETX	0.0096	0.0064	0.0046	0.0046	0.0190	0.0453	0.0627
from M1	0.0240	0.0208	0.0190	0.0190	0.0144	0.0407	0.0581
from M2	0.0503	0.0471	0.0453	0.0453	0.0407	0.0278	0.0458
from M3	0.0677	0.0645	0.0627	0.0627	0.0581	0.0468	0.0195

Figure 8.2

Anyone moving natural gas from one zone to another will have the same tariff terms defining transport cost. Market participants are on a level playing field when it comes to delivering natural gas to a particular zone. So, for example, moving natural gas from South Texas (STX) to TETM3 (M3) costs $0.0677/MMBtu, in addition to capacity charges which are defined in a similar fashion. Transport between two meters within M3 costs $0.0195. The use of zones in tariffs reduces the challenge of reliable price formation to a tractable number of locations.

- Hubs and Pools

A third organizing principle is that of hubs and pools. It is clear from Figure 5.2 that there are many pipelines. Being that these are on a two-dimensional surface, some are bound to intersect. Hubs and pools are essentially locations where multiple pipelines intersect (usually with associated storage nearby) and high volumes of both physical flows and trading are common. Figure 8.3 shows the area around Leidy hub where several pipelines are in close proximity, notably Transco (short for Transcontinental), Dominion and TCO.

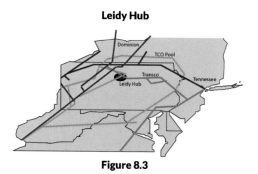

Figure 8.3

You can buy natural gas at a hub and receive delivery from any of the pipelines with meters at the hub. The oft mentioned Henry Hub is at the intersection of 13 pipelines. Figure 8.4 shows commonly referenced trading hubs and pools.

Figure 8.4

We will explore the various regions shown here in more detail below.

- Backhauls

Most major pipelines have a typical direction of flow. In the case of pipelines supplying the northeast from the Gulf Coast, for many years the flow was almost always from south to north—warm to cold. This natural orientation results in the concept of "backhaul", which occurs when someone transports gas against the prevailing flow on the pipeline, for example from TETM3 to South Texas (M3 to STX in Figure 8.2). A backhaul is not a physical flow of gas; it is transport through displacement, also referred to as a "paper flow," from an upstream point to a downstream point. Molecules are not literally flowing backwards; rather the overall south-to-north flow in this example is reduced by the amount of backhaul occurring. Pipelines do not typically charge for backhauling, and this is reasonable. All that a backhaul does is reduce the amount of gas that the pipeline has to support, so if anything backhauls should be rewarded for alleviating congestion on a pipeline.

Shale gas, and particularly the development of the Marcellus field in the Northeast, has changed the natural flows on some pipelines. Production in the greater Northeast is now so large as to render a natural flow direction somewhat moot. TETCO filed for a change in tariff structure with the FERC in October 2012 requesting approval to assess fuel charges on all transactions in their system. In the application TETCO indicated that, as a result of Marcellus production, it has experienced significant changes in customer sourcing patterns across its system that are at variance with historical flow patterns, and that it is unable to reliably identify which individual transactions are flow reducers (backhauls). The result of this change in tariff is manifest in the symmetry in transport costs in Figure 8.2—flows between zones now sustain the same usage charges in both directions.

- Scheduling

The flow of natural gas within a zone has its own complexities. Gas is not delivered to a zone but rather to a meter within a zone. Suppose, for example, that you have purchased natural gas from one of the usual dealers, say BP, for delivery in the TETCO M3 zone. Your gas scheduler contacts the BP scheduler and confirms the trade and specifies, for example, that you would like the natural gas delivered to the meter 70949 at Hanover, NJ. This meter is located within the zone in question, and defines exactly where you want to take delivery. The BP scheduler then informs your scheduler of the transport contract number on which the natural gas will be nominated. On the day of delivery your scheduler monitors the pipeline EBB (the bulletin board) to verify that the correct volume of natural gas was delivered on that contract number to the 70949 meter.

In this example, if the original trade was in the form of a *monthly* purchase, such as physical basis or index (discussed later in this chapter), the same volume, referred to as the "base load", would be delivered on a daily basis throughout the month. For the typical *daily* cash market transaction delivery would only occur on the following day.

Price Formation and Basis Risk

Zones and hubs not only simplify transport pricing and contract mechanics, but also make spot price formation possible. Indices are constructed at the more commonly traded zones and hubs, with vendors surveying trading activity to construct representative prices; Figure 3.1 was an example. These indices serve as settlement prices for financial trades as well as useful information for analysis of locational price risk.

By construction, supply and demand balance at any particular time and location—spot prices are the mechanism by which this is accomplished. If supply and demand were slowly varying and predictable, spot prices would not fluctuate very much. Long term trends in production and consumption are arguably predictable; short term weather-driven fluctuations in demand and infrastructure failure are the primary factors driving spot price volatility.

- Temperature and Pipeline Constraints

Spot basis is often heavily dependent on the effects that temperature has on demand. This is particularly true in the regions of the country in which high heating demand is in play in the winter. An example of this appears in Figure 8.5 which shows the ratio of TETM3 spot prices to those at Henry Hub versus the average daily temperature at La Guardia (KLGA) for the period 2011-2013. Many tariffs, including TETCO, have a fuel component, which means transport costs will systematically increase with price level, making price ratios a reasonable way to view basis relationships.

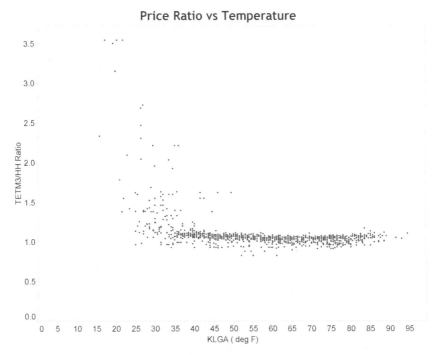

Figure 8.5

Extremely high price levels relative to Henry Hub are almost exclusively a low temperature phenomenon.

Figure 8.6 is another view of this behavior. The top plot shows the average percentage premium (or discount when negative) of TETM3 spot prices to those of Henry Hub by temperature decile—the lowest decile labelled "1", for example, exhibited an average premium of roughly 45%. The lower plot shows the standard deviation. The same 2011-2013 time period was used.

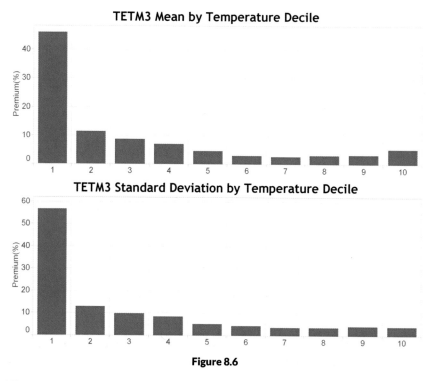

Figure 8.6

The most striking feature in this figure is the very large price ratios (and standard deviations) at the coldest temperatures. This is a common theme in the Northeast, where high population density and heating requirements routinely push daily winter demand orders of magnitude higher than the annual average. Storage withdrawals are used to meet some of the demand spikes, but often large volumes must be transported from elsewhere, particularly the Gulf region, to balance the system. This causes spot prices at the demand sinks to rise relative to lower cost (at least during the winter) supply in the Gulf.

Major Northeast Pipelines

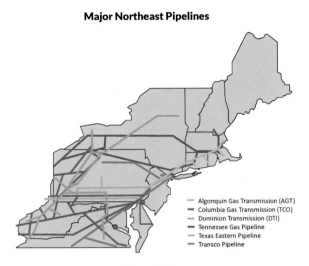

Figure 8.7

Figure 8.7 is a stylized depiction of the pipeline system in the Northeast. The purpose of this system is, generally speaking, to move gas to the Northeast from surplus areas further south. When transport capacity becomes limited, either due to high demand or mechanical problems, spot prices can spike.

Anecdotal discussion of what drives price blowouts complement statistical analysis, and help shed light on the underlying drivers. Looking back at Figure 3.1, in December 2007 extremely cold weather, compounded by what some market participants would later describe in an over-used cliché as a "perfect storm" of constraints on pipelines, resulted in price increases across the Northeast and well beyond. The confluence of events included compressor failures in pipes carrying gas from the Gulf and outages in the production fields in Sable Island that sends gas into New England from Canada. Another strong move in the spot markets occurred in December 2010 through January 2011 when compressor problems on Texas Eastern in conjunction with cold weather caused a pronounced jump in spot prices. There are many potential points of failure in the system, and infrastructure problems are hard to predict.

All of the episodes above involved cold weather and equipment problems. The Polar Vortex of 2014 provides an even more striking example, remarkable since these extremely high prices occurred when the system was functioning properly. Figure 8.8 shows prices at three primary delivery points[42] in the greater Northeast during Jan2014, a month which saw prolonged periods of very low temperatures.

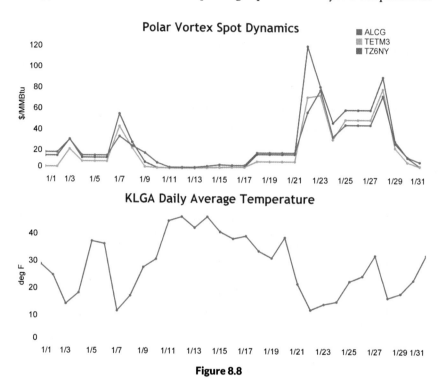

Figure 8.8

Low temperatures prevailed across the entire eastern seaboard, resulting in competition for fuel that drove cash prices to levels never seen before, without the usual culprit of pipeline problems. There was simply more demand than the system could handle.

- *The Impact of Supply Imbalances*

Large price spikes are the sensational feature of natural gas prices, making and breaking companies with unhedged positions in a matter of days. There

---

42 ALCG is Algonquin citygate, and TZ6NY denotes Transco Zone 6 New York.

are also, however, the slow but persistent trends that lack headline appeal, but which can be more impressive in their ultimate impact. Shale gas is such an example. The continuing secular increase in production in several key regions in the U.S. has resulted in changes in price relationships that are arguably more disruptive than polar vortices.

In Figure 8.6 we used the earlier date range 2011-2013 for a reason—this period predates much of the shale onslaught. Figure 8.9 shows the same plot using 2014-2016—and some very important differences can be seen.

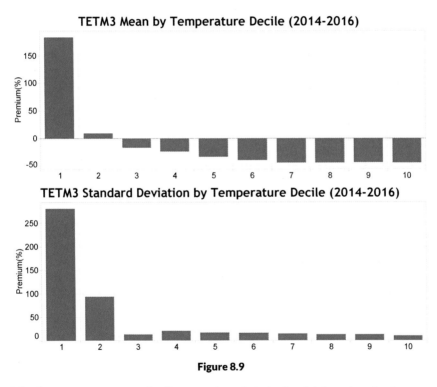

Figure 8.9

The low temperature volatility remains—it is in fact higher than in the earlier plot due to the inclusion of the polar vortex period. Of greater interest, however, is the systematic discount at all but the lowest temperatures; a discount approaching a remarkable 50% at the higher deciles. The minimum price during this period for TETM3 was approximately $0.38/MMBtu, almost free natural gas, and certainly a price far below production costs.

Such discounts to Henry Hub, which would have been considered unthink-able a few years earlier, is due primarily to Marcellus shale gas in Pennsylva-nia[43]. As Marcellus production increased without enough pipeline capacity to transport the gas out of the region, many Northeast basis locations expe-rienced a huge price collapse and are at present trading at a *discount* to Henry Hub, at least for much of the year. Figure 8.10 shows TETM3 and NYMEX forward curves on two dates. The world was quite accustomed to the situa-tion shown in the top plot. Six years later, although the winter premium still persists, the TETM3 discount over most of the year is market confirmation of the regional changes in production.

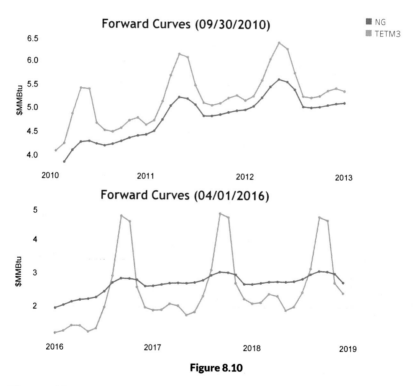

Figure 8.10

The world is not standing still, though. Markets tend to equilibrate, and the collapse in price is spawning the development of additional pipeline capacity out of the region into neighboring premium basis locations. During the injec-tion season (Apr-Oct) of 2016, the average discount of TETM3 spot prices

43 This change also supports the TETCO petition for the change in the tariff structure mentioned earlier.

to Henry Hub was roughly -$1.17/MMBtu; the daily TETM3 to Henry Hub spot price ratio was roughly 55%. Figure 8.11 shows TETM3 / Henry Hub forward price ratios in April 2016 and 2017. Note that the values for Apr-Oct 2016 were not too far off of what ultimately prevailed. By 2017, however, this ratio is now over 80% due to the fact that traders are aware of new pipeline capacity capable of pulling gas from the eastern markets and sending it west during surplus months. Systems adapt and trading shops are paying attention.

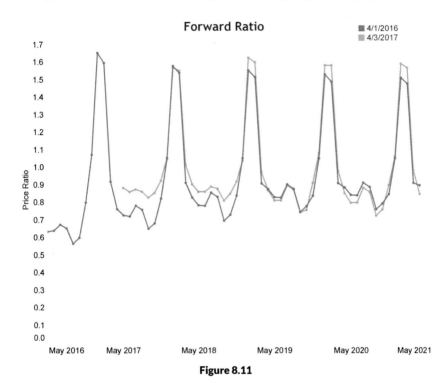

Figure 8.11

- Variations by Region

Spot price dynamics can vary meaningfully from region to region. In the previous section we started with the Northeast due to the rich nature of spot price dynamics and its continuing gyrations in response to both extreme weather events and shale production. From a trading perspective, however, it is the Gulf region that remains the fulcrum of U.S. natural gas markets.

For many years Gulf production constituted the bulk of the U.S. total. Infrastructure was built to gather and move gas to other parts of the country, and it was a natural place to create a benchmark back in the early 1990s when the NYMEX contract was launched. The Gulf can be thought of as everything in proximity to Henry Hub, spanning Florida to parts of Texas, and hosting a number of commonly traded pricing points.

The statistical behavior of basis within the greater Gulf region is very different than what we saw in the Northeast, due to markedly lower heating demand and shorter transport distances. Figure 8.12 shows the response of Houston Ship Channel (a major trading hub) spot basis by temperature decile from 2014-2016, but in this case using KIAH (Houston) daily average temperatures.

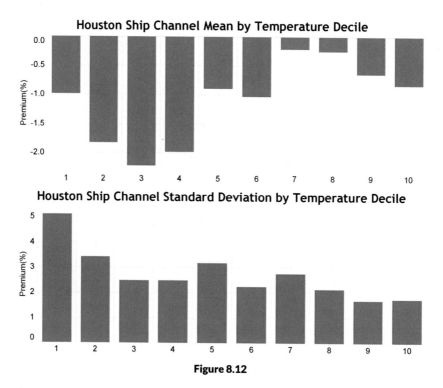

Figure 8.12

The point of this figure is to show the close coupling of Houston Ship Channel and Henry Hub across all temperatures, with a relatively small discount—of the order of a few percentage points.

Other noteworthy regions in the U.S. include:

- Mid-Continent: This region is just west of the Gulf, and includes the Texas panhandle and Oklahoma. The El Paso Permian hub, which appears in Figure 8.4, is in an area that supports significant production from both shale and coal bed methane fields. Statistical behavior is similar to that shown in Figure 8.12 for Houston Ship Channel, with generally a slightly larger discount due to production.
- Midwest: This is the other region with high heating demand. The two most commonly traded delivery locations are Chicago and Michcon citygates. Statistically, spot price behavior is similar to the Northeast in the winter, with large basis premia, but without the major discount at higher temperatures.
- Rockies: This region, which covers much of Utah, Colorado and Wyoming, hosts significant production, both conventional and coal bed methane. The primary pricing points are Rockies, Kern and Opal. The Rockies provide another dramatic example of the large changes in supply and demand that can occur over only a few years. Figure 8.13 shows Rockies spot basis starting in the early 2000s. The lowest price was $0.22 / MMBtu, and the minimum basis seen was over $7 / MMBtu discount to Henry Hub. Natural gas was effectively free in the Rockies at this time because of high levels of production and the fact that it was hard to get it anywhere. During this period, forward prices at Rockies collapsed, creating an incentive to build transport. A new equilibrium of sorts was established near the end of the decade with the completion of the Rockies Express pipeline, which opened demand centers in the Midwest to Rockies supply. Our now standard view is shown in Figure 8.14 in which Denver was used as the reference temperature. These are far from the eye-popping discounts seen in mid-2000s—evidence that infrastructure buildout has helped balance the system.

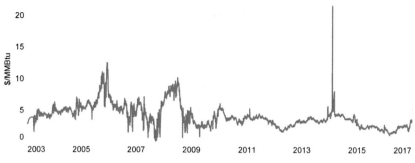

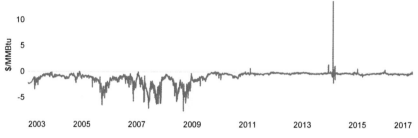

Figure 8.13

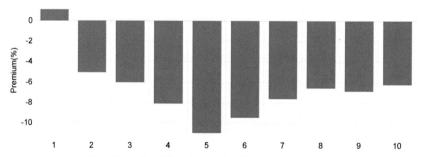

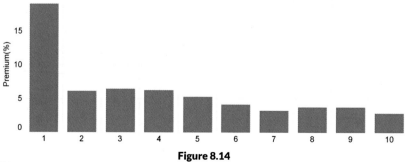

Figure 8.14

- West: We conclude with the Western U.S., with major pricing points being SoCal in southern California, PGE citygate near San Francisco, and Sumas near the Canadian border in Washington state. This is a large swathe of territory—in fact, many traders would view the northwest and southwest as altogether distinct regions. SoCal in the southwest has a response to summer electricity demand arising from air conditioning requirements—this is clearly visible in Figure 8.15 which shows price statistics versus KLAS (Las Vegas). For comparison Figure 8.16 shows PGE spot price statistics, pertinent to delivery in San Francisco further north, in reference to Sacramento temperature. Here prices are systematically premium to Henry Hub, with heating demand increases more pronounced relative to SoCal, and the air conditioning response more muted.

SoCal Mean by Temperature Decile

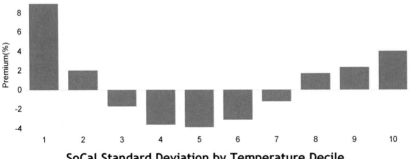

SoCal Standard Deviation by Temperature Decile

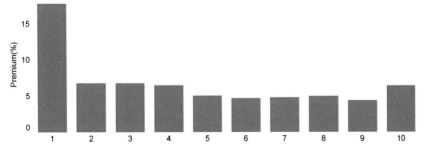

Figure 8.15

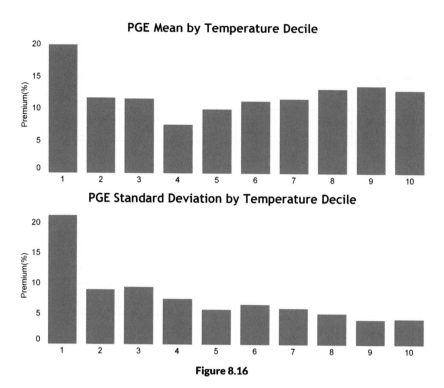

Figure 8.16

The main point of this digression into the idiosyncrasies of locational prices is that details in the supply and demand profiles of a region matter. In fact, we have barely scratched the surface in this short survey—a qualified regional basis desk would be analyzing inventory, pipe flows and production statistics in extraordinary detail, using such information in conjunction with detailed knowledge of the pipeline systems to craft trading strategies. We turn next to how portfolio management decisions are implemented.

Trading Locational Price Risk

The challenge in basis trading is making effective use of liquidity at the NG benchmark futures to hedge risks at less liquid locations. This is analogous to the problem of hedging long tenor risk, where liquidity is limited, by using near dated contracts via the stack-and-roll hedging protocol discussed in the previous chapter. Here the focus will be on locational, or basis spreads.

There are dozens of delivery locations at which trading occurs to some extent, and far more at which natural gas is delivered. Daily trading volume at even the most liquid locations, however, is typically well below that seen in the Henry Hub futures and swaps markets, simply due to diffusion of commercial activity across all of these delivery points. Limitations in liquidity can make hedging a challenging affair.

It is common for basis traders to find themselves with a sizable position, long or short, at an illiquid delivery location. This situation can arise in different ways. A natural gas retailer may have just closed on an acquisition of a portfolio of end users. Alternatively, a dealer may have just provided a hedge, either by selling gas to an end user, such as an electricity generator or buying it from a producer.

Regardless of origin, if you have a risk position at a particular location that is large relative to the amount of trading that usually occurs there, the problem that you confront is finding an efficient way to hedge your price exposure. In some cases you will be lucky, finding another counterparty who is bidding or offering exactly what you need. However, it is much more likely that you will have to pay bid/offer spreads to get things done. The larger your position and the more rapidly you try to hedge it, the higher the transaction costs.

Hedging decisions are a matter of time-scale. The longer you are willing to hold a particular risk, the more slowly and efficiently you can execute your hedging program without moving the markets and paying large transaction costs.

- Working Example

To illustrate the variety of ways in which a basis position can be hedged, consider the situation in which you are short five-a-day at TETM3 in your natural gas book at a fixed price of $6.20 in the month of Jan18. The current date is 03Apr2017.

If you took no action, then the economics of your position are as shown in Figure 8.17.

Unhedged Customer Basis Position

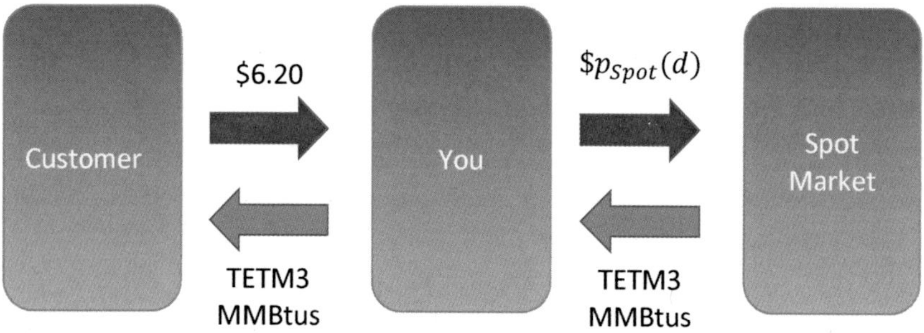

Figure 8.17

You will receive the $6.20/MMBtu from the customer; in return, on a daily basis you must procure the required gas at the price available to you, which we have denoted as p_{spot}.

We will now explore several ways in which this position can be hedged.

- Fixed Price Physical Hedge

The simplest hedge is to buy TETM3 for physical delivery. On 03Apr2017 the TETM3 forward price for Jan18 was $5.58[44]. Suppose that during the day

---

44 This was the ICE settlement price for this contract on that date. It can be thought of as a roughly the mid-market price prevailing at that time—we say roughly since the price was no doubt varying over the course or the trading day.

you bought the full five-a-day at $5.83. This premium to $5.58 is intended to reflect the extra money you pay to purchase this rather large quantity of natural gas in a single trade. Your resulting position is shown in Figure 8.18.

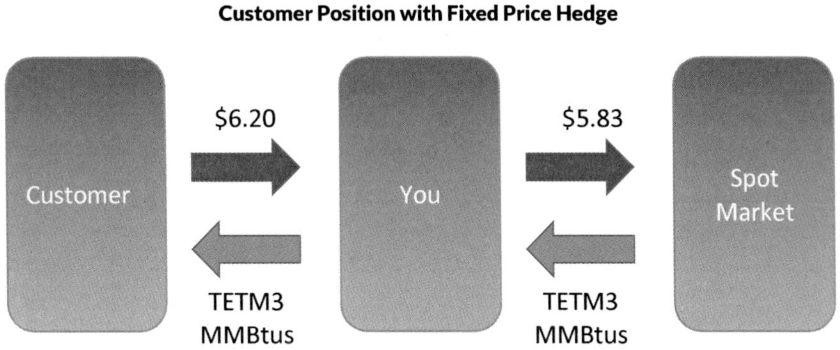

Customer Position with Fixed Price Hedge

Figure 8.18

As before you receive the $6.20/MMBtu from the customer, but now you have acquired the natural gas at a fixed price. Your price risk is fully mitigated. If between now and the delivery month the price for Jan18 were to increase dramatically, which would lower the value of your customer sale, the value of the hedge would increase commensurately.

- Fixed Price Financial Hedge

Another hedge, similar in simplicity to the physical hedge, is the financial version in which you buy the TETM3 Gas Daily futures. Instead of receiving physical delivery, you are paid the Gas Daily index. Assume that you purchase the required five-a-day of GD futures at $5.78. Your resulting position is shown in Figure 8.19.

Customer Position with GD Futures Hedge

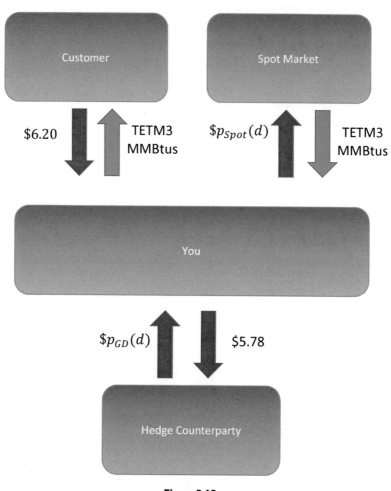

Figure 8.19

The situation is slightly more complex due to the fact that at delivery you still need to go out into the spot market and acquire the gas. There is no guarantee that the price that you will pay each day will be identical to the Gas Daily index. While you can generally purchase physical gas at GD, the price usually includes a spread to the index. Moreover, large volumes can be hard to transact in this way. The upshot is that there is usually a residual risk due to the daily difference between the price at which you actually purchase the gas and the GD index: $p_{spot} - p_{GD}$.

It is worth emphasizing a point made earlier in Chapter 6. The hedge slippage arising from $p_{spot} - p_{GD}$ is a relatively small risk only insofar as the index is well-designed and in a liquid trading location. Otherwise, the actual price that you pay to acquire the gas can end up being quite different from what you receive based upon an index price derived from a survey of only a few trades that occurred that day. In our example, TETM3 is relatively liquid and price surveys are generally viewed as consistent with actual trading.

- Hedge Decomposition—Benchmark and Basis

Either of the two approaches above result in a comfortably hedged position. Moreover, you are not displeased with the result; after all, you have locked in a profit. This last fact, however, assumed that you had a customer paying you a healthy premium to current market prices; a premium that exceeded the transaction costs. Had this price been lower, you would have less margin (margin being the difference between the customer price and current mid-market prices) available to pay hedge costs, not to mention the salaries of your staff and other operational costs. Moreover, if liquidity had been lighter on the hedging date, you could end up blowing through the entire margin altogether using either of these hedging programs.

It is very common for limitations in liquidity to render the costs of fixed price hedges untenable. In such situations, a natural way to organize your thoughts is to view your risk as being comprised of two components. The first is the overall price level risk, represented by benchmark Henry Hub prices; the second is the basis risk arising from changes in the price spread between the particular delivery location and Henry Hub. Over the course of a single hour or day, it is usually the price level risk that is dominant.

Figure 8.20 shows the standard deviation of changes of locational prices over 5 business days (selected as a plausible hedging time-horizon) at a few of the delivery locations that we have discussed earlier. The component that can be attributed to Henry Hub price changes is labelled "Benchmark". This can be thought of as the risk that could be hedged using Henry Hub futures. The remaining risk is labelled "Basis." Hedging this component requires trades with the relevant locational price exposure[45].

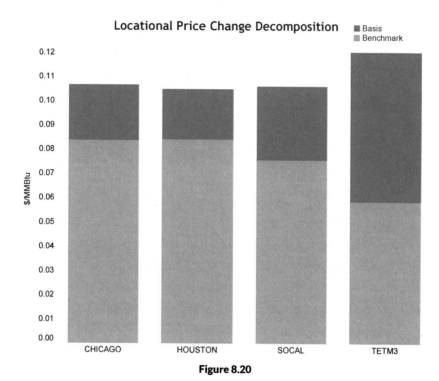

Figure 8.20

The essential fact is that a Henry Hub hedge will substantially reduce price exposure in all cases.

These results point to a sensible hedging strategy involving the following steps:

- Hedge at the benchmark: Use the Henry Hub futures markets to quickly and efficiently eliminate price level risk;
- Hedge the basis : Proceed to reduce your locational exposure by trading basis spreads to Henry Hub.

---

45 The time period was 2015-2016, and the prices used were rolling calendar strips. Absolute price changes were used here to provide a palpable $/MMBtu perspective.

- Fine tuning: Convert your hedge to the required price exposure—monthly or daily fixings.

This train of thought is analogous to stack-and-roll hedging for time spreads, in which initial hedges using shorter tenor contracts are subsequently rolled to longer tenors using calendar spreads.

Returning to our working example, on 03Apr2017 the settlement price for Henry Hub Jan18 futures was $3.547. Buying five-a-day is routine; daily NYMEX volume on that particular day was 12,258 or just under 400 contracts per day; and this is the volume on only one exchange. We will assume that this purchase occurs at $3.58; a much smaller premium than for the direct TETM3 purchase due to high liquidity.

By making the Henry Hub futures purchase, you have eliminated a substantial amount of price risk (recall Figure 8.20), and you have done so at a comparatively small transaction cost. However, the spread risk between TETM3 and Henry Hub remains. If you took no further action you would still be exposed to changes in basis between TETM3 and Henry Hub prior to the delivery month, as well as daily price risk through the delivery month since the Henry Hub position expires and ceases to do anything for you. Even if you took your futures hedge to physical delivery, you would receive Henry Hub spot prices in return for sale of the physical gas you received. The result would be daily exposure to the spread between TETM3 and Henry Hub spot prices—the spread risk remains.

We turn next to the second and third steps of the hedging program, in which these initial NG futures hedges are transformed into exactly what you need to hedge your physical short position.

Note: In practice the trades discussed next are usually transacted as futures on any of the usual exchanges. However, our presentation below will refer to swaps because the resulting cash flows are simple and avoid the technical issue of daily cash flows resulting from margining. From a hedging perspective these are functionally equivalent.

- Basis Trades

The Henry Hub futures expire three business days prior to the contract month, at which time a final settlement price for delivery is posted—we have referred to this before as LD (for "last day"). Basis trades provide a mechanism to buy or sell the spread between a similar monthly price fixing at a particular delivery location and the LD price at Henry Hub, thereby transferring price risk at Henry Hub to the desired location.

The reference monthly settlement price for a basis trade is usually the Inside FERC (or IFERC) index published by Platts[46]. Like the daily GD prices used earlier, the IFERC index is established via a survey of physical trading activity. In the case of IFERC, however, it is the volumetric weighted average price of physical trades reported during the last five trading days prior to the delivery month. These five days are referred to as "bid week"[47].

When you buy a basis swap you will receive the IFERC (or IF) index and you will pay the sum of the LD price of the NG futures contract and a spread—the spread being the basis price at the time of the transaction. Figure 8.21 shows the cash flows in the context of our working example, where we assume that on the trade date 03Apr2017 the basis swap was transacted at a spread of $2.08. This means that at the end of the bid-week preceding Jan18 all cash flows are known and are as shown in Figure 8.21.

---

46 Another vendor that provides monthly index settles is Natural Gas Intelligence, also referred to as NGI.
47 In the Alberta natural gas market AECO, the averaging period consists of the trading days in the previous month, hence is more aptly described as "bid month".

Basis Futures Cash Flows

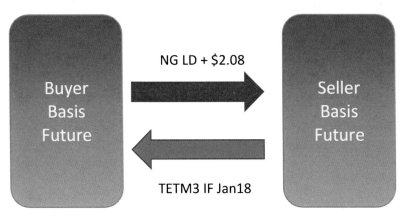

Figure 8.21

Suppose, for example, that the NG swap contract expires at $3.95 and the bid-week price is posted as $6.37. The settlement amount is the difference between the IF price and the LD price adjusted by the spread at which you transacted:

$$\$6.37 - (\$3.95 + \$2.08) = \$0.34 \text{ / MMBtu}$$

The $2.08 is the price at which you transacted the basis swap. Note that in this example the final spread between TETM3 and Henry Hub was: $6.37 - $3.95 = $2.42, which was substantially greater than the prevailing level of $2.08 at the time you did the hedge. This is why your basis swap yielded a profit, insulating your short position against the increase in the price of TETM3 relative to Henry Hub.

Paired with the original Henry Hub trade, you now have a portfolio that is largely hedged to locational price risk. Figure 8.22 shows the resulting situation in which you:

- Receive the fixed price from the customer.
- Procure natural gas at the daily spot price.
- Receive the IF index and pay the sum of the Henry Hub purchase and the basis swap spread.

The last payment stream is the net result of the NG fixed price trade and the basis swap, also shown in the figure.

Customer Position with Basis Futures Hedge

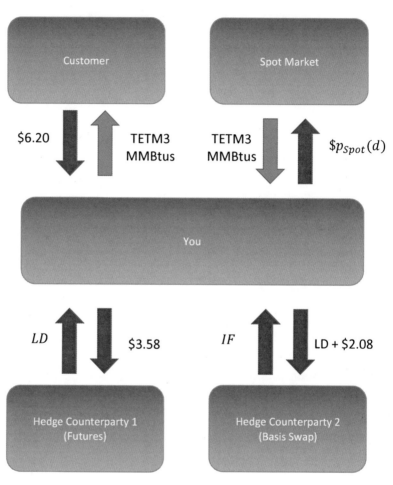

Figure 8.22

These cash flows are also summarized in Table 8.1 (note that we have put the IF receivable on the Pay/Deliver side in the Total).

Transaction	Receive	Pay/Deliver
Customer	$6.20	MMBtus
Spot Market	MMBtus	p_{spot}
Futures	LD	$3.58
Basis Swap	IF	LD + $2.08
Total	$6.20	$5.66+ $p_{spot} - IF$

Table 8.1: Cash Flows with Basis Swap Hedge

The punchline is that your residual risk now consists of the difference between the daily spot price and the IF index, which fixes at the beginning of the month: $p_{spot} - IF$. You are now hedged for basis price risk up to the delivery month; beyond that your position remains exposed to daily price fluctuations which require index swaps to hedge.

- Index Trades

Index futures provide a way to buy or sell the spread between spot prices and first-of-month indices such as those published by IFERC and NGI. These are the trades used in the final step in our hedge program that started with Henry Hub futures, and subsequently transferred price risk to a specific location via basis trades. This last step will utilize index trades to hedge the risk associated with the spread between basis indices and daily spot prices.

It may be tempting to think that the risk involved in holding the spread between daily spot prices and monthly indices is small. After all, only a few days separate bid week and subsequent delivery day. However, we have seen that spot prices can vary wildly from day to day (recall Figure 3.1).

Figure 8.23 illustrates this point. Each bar is the average absolute spread between daily spot prices and the forward price for the delivery month just before expiry (a good proxy for indices such as IFERC) for three delivery locations: Henry Hub, TETM3 in the New York City area and Algonquin City Gate (ALCG), which is further north near Boston.

Daily versus Monthly Price Risk

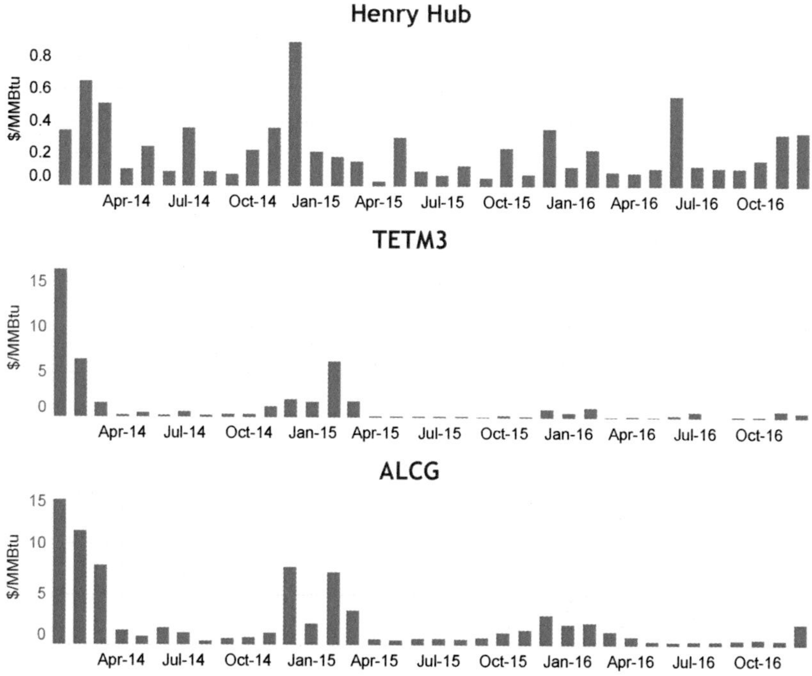

Figure 8.23

Note the difference in scale between the Henry Hub results, with maximum values under $1/MMBtu, and the Northeastern locations with this price risk sustaining levels above $15/MMBtu.

To get a closer look at the non-winter months, Figure 8.24 shows the results for 2016.

Daily versus Monthly Price Risk (2016)

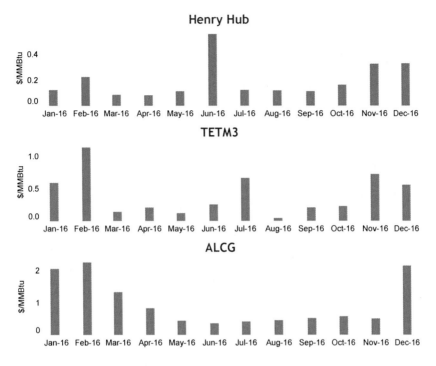

Figure 8.24

Typical fluctuations are still of the order of $0.50/MMBtu, even in the more temperate months, and several multiples higher in some cases. Price risk of this magnitude cannot be ignored—or rather, you ignore it at your peril. For perspective, the daily consumption of large combined cycle generator is roughly 10 lots per day. A fluctuation of 50 cents in gas price is equivalent to $50K. For many asset owners and physical gas marketers this risk is large enough to matter. This is why index futures are traded.

Index futures are similar to the GD swaps, but with one modification: while the first leg remains a daily index, the second leg is replaced by a monthly index such as IFERC. When you buy an index future you receive the difference between GD and the IFERC index plus a spread. Figure 8.25 depicts the cash flows of a long index swap position related to our working example. In this figure the holder of the long position (you) will receive p_{spot} and pay IF + $0.05.

Index Futures Cash Flows

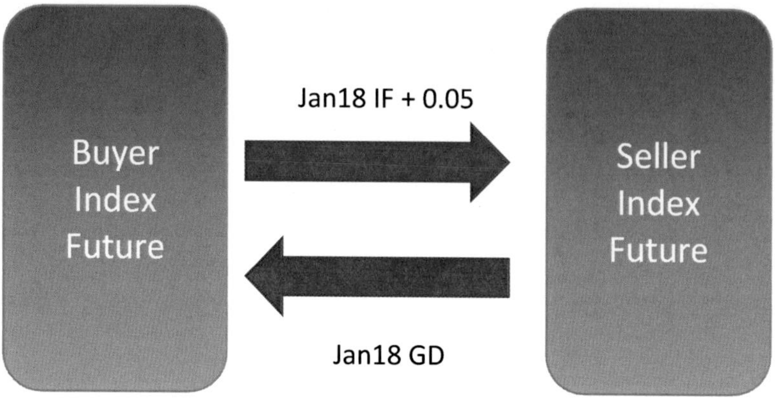

Figure 8.25

The five cent adder should be thought of as the trade price. At the time that you wanted to buy this index swap, the market for the Jan18 TETM3 index swap would have looked something like: bid at $0.03 and offer at $0.05. You transacted at the offer side in this figure.

Prior to the start of bid week, both legs of an index swap are unknown; both are "floating" legs and your "overall" price risk is essentially flat. Technically speaking, you are long GD and short IFERC in our example. However, in the absence of any short term information about the delivery month, such as weather forecasts or pipe flow information, these two legs are tightly coupled, with relatively small changes due to the ebb and flow of trading activity. The two legs are, after all, just different indices for the price of natural gas at the same location and the same delivery month—the only difference being that one is established before the month starts, the other throughout the month on a daily basis.

After bid week, however, the IFERC leg is fixed, so that you are now long GD against a fixed price. The risk of an index future, therefore, evolves during the lifecycle of the trade. During bid week, each trading day that passes establishes some fraction of what will ultimately be the final IFERC price. At the end of bid week, just before delivery starts, the IFERC leg is fixed and you are now long a fixed price GD swap—the fixed price being the IFERC index which was just published plus the spread. During the delivery month, the GD delta amortizes off uniformly by delivery day.

The implication is that over the course of bid week the net price exposure (delta) of the index trade grew from zero to the full notional. If you knew in advance that trade volume was uniform over the five days, then each day one fifth of the index is established and you would be longer by one fifth of the total volume. Trading over bid week is not, however, uniformly distributed—there is typically more trading activity in the first three days of bid week due to the fact that after the third day the benchmark NG futures has expired[48].

Changes to your position continue into the delivery month. As the delivery month progresses, each day yields a settlement at the prevailing GD price, and the residual length decreases by the daily volume of the basis futures. The risk profile of an index futures contract is depicted in Figure 8.26.

Risk Profile of Index Futures

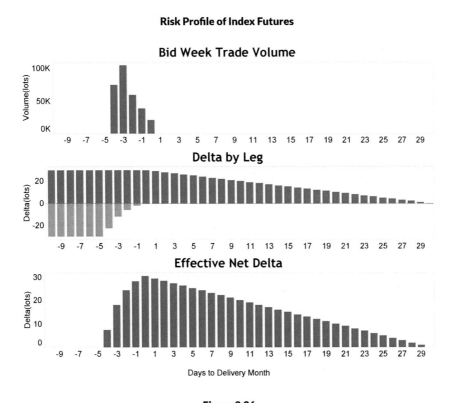

Figure 8.26

---

48 While it is possible make statistical estimates of bid-week trading volumes by day, most risk systems treat the fixing using a simple mechanism, one such being uniform fixing over bid-week.

The top plot shows hypothetical volumes of trading activity indexed by the number of days to the delivery month. The middle plot shows the delta of the respective legs, and the bottom plot shows the effective net delta, viewing IF and GD risk as identical for the unfixed components of each.

Returning to our working example, the purchase of 5 contracts per day of the index swap yields the set of cash flows depicted in Figure 8.27.

Customer Position with Basis and Index Hedges

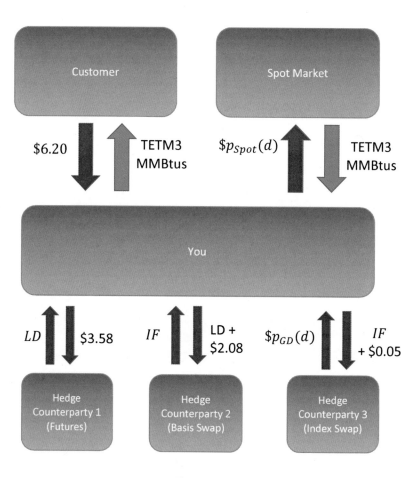

Figure 8.27

This figure looks complex, but this is simply due to the fact that three distinct trades were used to synthesize a fixed price gas daily swap.

Table 8.2 also portrays the cash flows for this now complete hedge; it is identical to Table 8.1 aside from the one row showing the index swap. The residual risk has now been reduced to the spread between the daily spot price for physical delivery and the GD index, exactly as in the GD financial hedge represented in Figure 8.19.

Transaction	Receive	Pay/Deliver
Customer	$6.20	MMBtus
Spot Market	MMBtus	p_{spot}
Futures	LD	$3.58
Basis Swap	IF	LD + $2.08
Index Swap	p_{GD}	IF + $0.05
Total	$6.20	$5.71 + p_{spot} - p_{GD}

Table 8.2: Cash Flows with Basis and Index Swap Hedge

- *Physical Basis and Index Trades*

The examples above involved trades that were financially settled. In each case hedge slippage took the form of the as yet unknown price for you to actually procure the required physical gas (p_{spot}) and the price defining the financially offsetting cost (IF or p_{GD}). There are, however, physical versions of each of the trades above which result in physical delivery and eliminate the inherent slippage between daily physical purchases and financial replicas.

In a physical basis trade, the buyer receives physical natural gas ratably over the delivery month and pays the sum of the LD futures price and a spread as shown in Figure 8.28.

Physical Basis Trade

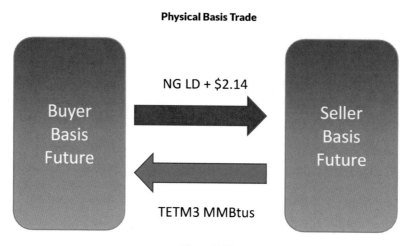

Figure 8.28

This is analogous to the basis swap, the only difference being that rather than receiving the IF index, the buyer of physical basis receives MMBtus.

In our working problem, you could have purchased physical basis at $2.14, which we have set at a small premium to the basis swap executed earlier (see Figure 8.22), which is typical. In this case your position would be as shown in Figure 8.29 with physical delivery at a fixed price—the sum of the prices of the futures and the physical basis transaction prices.

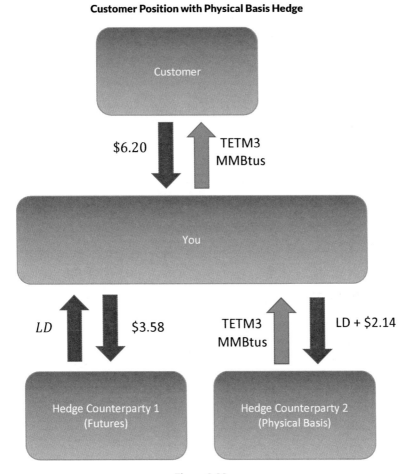

Customer Position with Physical Basis Hedge

Figure 8.29

Physical index, the last of the trade types discussed in this chapter, serve a similar purpose as physical basis, but against a locational monthly index. For example, the buyer of a physical index receives MMBtus and pays a spread to the IF index at the location in question. As with physical basis, a physical index trade can be used instead of an index swap to convert the final leg of the hedge sequence shown in Figure 8.27 to physical delivery. In this case the spot transaction and the index trade in Figure 8.27 would be replaced with a single physical index trade.

Given the purity of the resulting risk position using physical basis and index trades, it is fair to ask why anyone would use financial hedges—the basis and index swaps. The reason is liquidity and cost. Financial participants add to liquidity; moreover, it is typical for a premium to be charged for physical delivery. Your decision about which hedging strategy to deploy remains, for all practical purposes, a judgment call.

CHAPTER 9

Options

NATURAL GAS MARKETS are relatively mature. Options and structured transactions are standard fare for many trading desks and end users
alike. For natural gas, and physical commodities markets broadly, optionality embedded in physical assets drives options markets. The details of the
types of options that are created may vary between commodities and the
various types of assets within each market, but the theme of infrastructure
as the origin of physical options pertains broadly.

Anytime a pipeline is built, an option of sorts is created. If the spot price of natural gas at the delivery point exceeds the price at the source by more than the
variable cost to transport the gas, then it makes sense to use the pipeline to move
the gas; otherwise it does not. The pipeline is, therefore, essentially a call option
on the price spread, with the strike being the (variable) cost of transport[49]. In
fact, the pipeline is, at least to first approximation, a collection (or strip) of daily
call options on the spread spanning the life of the asset. The price of this option,
referred to as the option premium, is the cost to build the pipeline.

There are, of course, complexities in any physical option. A pipeline is not
exactly a set of daily call options. Engineering attributes, the structure of
tariffs and contractual arrangements often mutate the exact nature of the
optionality that is embedded in the asset. But the theme is clear—a pipeline
gives the owner flexibility and hence optionality.

---

49 We are assuming that the reader is acquainted with standard options vernacular—a call (put) option
being the right, but not the obligation, to buy (sell) something at a specified price.

The same concept applies to storage, but in a slightly different way. Owners of a storage facility have the ability to buy natural gas for injection, leaving them with flexibility as to when they withdraw it for sale into the spot market. Storage is, therefore, an option, the value of which depends on the price of natural gas at different delivery times. It is in fact an exceptionally complex option. To simplify matters, however, suppose you were told you had access to a storage facility, with a restriction—you can inject gas in June and withdraw it the following January. Viewed from the perspective of some earlier time (before June), this is a call option on the spread between the price of natural gas in January and that in June. If this spread, properly adjusted for storage costs and funding rates, is big enough, it makes sense to inject in June and withdraw in January; otherwise it does not. Storage is, therefore, closely related to options on time spreads. As with pipelines, when developers build storage facilities, they are creating options.

Optionality arises at even more basic levels. Earlier we discussed how producers commonly hedge their anticipated production using swaps and futures. There is, however, a little more to the story. If the price of natural gas, as reflected in the appropriate forward curve, is above a producer's cost of production, fully inclusive of all engineering, development and funding costs, then it makes sense to drill and extract. If it isn't, it makes sense to wait. Natural gas fields are, in a sense, simply less flexible storage assets—natural gas is "stored" underground.

Physical infrastructure is not necessary for the existence of options markets—after all people can use options purely to leverage a speculative position. But these natural sources of optionality induce hedging activity related to the financing and development of physical assets, ultimately propelling the trading of options.

Commonly Traded Options

Natural gas markets support a broad array of options types, and, as with futures and swaps, it is useful to categorize them according to whether the price underlying an option is a futures contract, a daily spot index or a more complex set of multiple indices. Those options with futures prices as the underlying are usually either monthly or annual in nature in the sense of the delivery period of the underlying price. In contrast, those on spot indices usually involve daily exercise, with the value depending upon price volatility at short time scales. The third category with multiple underlying indices includes options on time spreads or basis spreads, as well as exotic structures with payoffs dependent on both spot prices and temperature. We will discuss a few of these in what follows.

- Monthly Options

The most commonly traded natural gas options are those directly related to the benchmark NG futures contracts. As such, these options are inherently monthly in nature. The key features are:

- Each option references a single delivery month and option expiry is typically four business days prior to the delivery month (penultimate expiration); this is one business day before the futures contract expires.
- European exercise is typical, especially on the CME, although American versions do trade. In the current protracted period of very low interest rates, there is usually little practical distinction between the two types, even at relatively long tenors.
- When an option involves financial settlement, the payoff is based on the difference between the futures settlement price on the day of exercise and the strike price.
- The most commonly traded options exercise directly into futures contracts.

Whether financially settled or exercising into futures, the payoff depends on the settlement price on the expiration date F_{exp} [50] the strike K and, of course, the option type.

- Call Payoff: $\max\left[F_{exp} - K, 0\right]$; you should only choose to buy gas at price K if it is below the prevailing market price: $K < F_{exp}$.
- Put Options: $\max\left[K - F_{exp}, 0\right]$; you will choose to sell natural gas at the strike K only if it is above the prevailing market price: $K > F_{exp}$.

Figure 9.1 illustrates the two payoffs as a function of the futures price at the time of exercise. This shows a short put struck at $K=2$ and a long call at $K=4$. The current market price is $3/MMBtu, and is represented by the linear swap payoff.

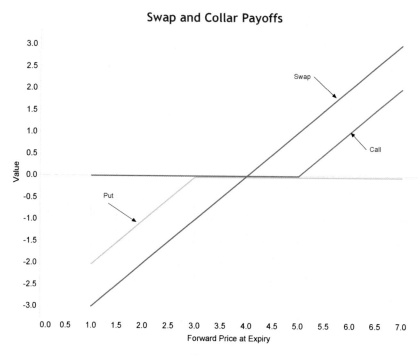

Figure 9.1

50 We are taking a little notational license here since in Chapter 6 we used the same notation for the settlement price at the expiration of the contract. Here we mean the settlement price on the date of option expiration.

The two options shown in Figure 9.1 together constitute what is referred to as a "collar" (or "fence" by some), with put and call positions of opposite sign and equal notional. If the strikes of the put and call are the same, the combined position would be identical to a swap[51]. Collars are very commonly traded in energy markets, and we will discuss them more later in this chapter.

To illustrate the mechanics of exercise, suppose that you were long 10 contracts of NYMEX NG Oct16 call options "struck at" (with a strike of) $2.50/MMBtu. On the expiration date 09/27/2016, four business days before the delivery month, you exercised the option. At this time you acquired a Oct16 futures contract at the strike price. That day the Oct16 contract was settled at $2.996, meaning that your margin account was credited $49,600, the product of the notional and the price difference. As of the time of exercise, you acquired a long position of 10 futures contracts, which you could choose to unwind or take to delivery.

For another example, suppose you were long 10 contracts of NYMEX NG Jan17 put options struck at $4.00/MMBtu. On 12/27/2016 you exercised the option. This means that during the day you sold a Jan17 futures contract at the strike price; the Jan17 contract was settled that day at $3.761. Your margin account was, therefore, credited $23,900. You are also short 10 futures contracts, which you could choose either to keep or to liquidate.

- Swaptions

A swaption is an option that can be exercised into a strip of underlying futures or swaps. Most swaptions that trade are annual, meaning that they exercise at a defined time before the start of a calendar year, and exercise results in a position in the associated calendar strip of futures contracts. Cash settled swaptions yield a payoff based on the difference between present value of the calendar strip (which is sum of the present values of each of the individual monthly positions) and the strike.

---

51 This fact yields the put-call parity relationship in which the difference between the value of a call and a put at the same strike must equal that of the resulting swap.

Annual swaptions are traded in situations where a hedger would like price protection over relatively long delivery periods. Swaptions are always cheaper than the analogous strip of monthly options for two reasons. First, the owner of a swaption can choose to exercise (or not, as the case may be) the entire strip of contracts at one time, as opposed to 12 distinct monthly exercises. Second, for all but the first contract month, exercise occurs well before that of the standard monthly option. So even if distinct exercise were allowed, the early exercise reduces the time value of the option.

- Daily Options

Options which reference daily spot indices are closely related to the daily swaps discussed in Chapter 6. The call or put payoff is applied to the difference between the daily price index and the strike.

One of the most common of these types of options settle on the GD index at a particular location. For example, a GD swap at \$5.50 for Jan18 at TETM3 yields a payoff equal to the sum of the daily differences of p_{spot} - 5.50, multiplied by the daily notional quantity. For the GD call, the payoff is based on the sum of $\max\left[p_{spot} - 5.50, 0\right]$.

Another class of daily options is very similar to the GD options, with one key difference—the fixed strike is replaced by a floating strike which sets at a FOM index, such as IFERC. These options, which are the moral equivalent of the index swaps of Chapter 6, are often referred to as GD/IFERC options. Continuing with the Jan18 setting, prior to bid week in late Dec17, the strike is floating just at it is for the associated index futures. If at the end of bid week the IFERC prints at \$6.10/MMBtu, then the call payoff becomes the same as a GD option payoff struck at \$6.10[52].

---

[52] In other asset classes such floating strike options are referred to as forward starters or Cliquet options.

- Options on Time Spreads

The parallels between swaps and options continues with options on time spreads, referred to as calendar spread options, or CSOs for short. In the most common form, the economics of exercise depends upon the spread between two distinct Henry Hub futures contracts, each with a different delivery month.

For example, a Henry Hub CSO put option on the CME for Oct18/Jan19 spread exercises into long Jan19 and short Oct18 futures positions on the date of standard option exercise for the Oct18 contract. Exercise is European. A cash settled version would settle against $F_{Jan18} - F_{Oct18}$ on this date. Call options are similar, but exercise into a short Jan19 and long Oct18 position.

- Options on Basis

Options on locational spreads, or basis options, are more commonly called pipe options. This name is presumably motivated by the fact that the economics of sourcing gas at one point on a pipeline and transporting it to another point is essentially a call option on a locational spread. Call options of this type can hedge, at least approximately, the value of transport.

In the most common version the relevant spread is the difference between IFERC bid-week index for a specified location and the Henry Hub contract expiration price, making these options analogous to basis futures. For example, an Oct18 Panhandle pipe option cash settles against the IFERC panhandle price for Oct18 and the last settlement price for the Oct18 Henry Hub futures, with the appropriate call or put payoffs applied.

Some Basic Facts

We now survey some important facts and terminology on options in the commodities setting; topics covered in much more detail in (Swindle, 2014). This section can be skipped by readers comfortable with option valuation and hedging concepts.

- Intrinsic Value and Moneyness

The intrinsic value of an option is the value that can be monetized immediately. For calls and puts this is the (discounted) value of the payoff at current market prices. For example, the intrinsic value of a call on a forward contract is: $d \max\left[F - K, 0\right]$ where F is the current forward price and d is the discount factor to the settlement date of the option. Options on futures do not require discounting, just as the present value of the futures contract did not. Extrinsic value is the remaining value of the option—the difference between the market value of the option value and its intrinsic value.

An out-of-the-money (OTM) option is one with zero intrinsic value. An in-the-money option (ITM) has positive intrinsic value. An at-the-money (ATM) option is one at the boundary of OTM and ITM options, where the strike is equal to the forward price. OTM calls (ITM puts) have strikes above the forward price $K>F$, and OTM puts (ITM calls) have strikes less than the forward price $K<F$.

- Early Exercise

Early exercise is never optimal for an American option on a forward contract. There is an easy way to see this, which is important to understand since it involves a simple hedging mechanism often invoked by traders.

Options on forward contracts settle at expiration of the contract, unlike for futures which are cash settled (margined) daily. Suppose that you have an American call option that is in-the-money $(F>K)$, and that you are tempted to exercise now to lock in the intrinsic value. Rather than exercise, you can sell the forward contract at the current market price F. The result is shown in Figure 9.2 where $K=3$ and $F=4$. The sale locks in the intrinsic value, and leaves you with an additional put payoff. It is the value of this OTM put that is being lost if you were to exercise early[53]. Traders commonly "swap" the ITM call for OTM puts and conversely.

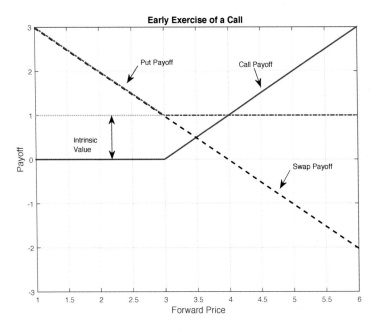

Figure 9.2

For American options on futures contracts, in contrast, early exercise can be optimal in some cases. This is due to the fact that options on futures are margined, and early exercise can yield cash now as opposed to a cash at a later time should you choose to defer exercise. Optimality of early exercise depends on the current price level, the tenor of the option, and interest rates; low interest rates reduce the incentive to exercise early.

---

53 This argument assumes that there are no transaction costs. In a market with high transaction costs, say at illiquid basis locations, the cost to execute the swap could exceed the value of the resulting put, making early exercise sensible.

- Risk Neutral Valuation

The topic of option pricing frameworks in commodities is expansive. Our goal here is to present only the bare essentials; a much broader discussion appears in, for example, (Swindle, 2014) (Eydeland, et al., 2003) and references therein. Moreover, the vast majority of traded options are relatively simple, and a common variation of basic Black-Scholes (referred to solely as Black, who modified the standard formulas to handle options on futures) is adequate for most purposes.

The underlying price in commodities options is a forward contract. Forward contracts do not require an initial cash investment, unlike say the purchase of a stock. Consequently, there is no cost of carry for any hedging strategy using forwards. As result, risk-neutral valuation requires that forward prices are drift free due to the absence of carrying costs, and Black-Scholes (officially Black-76, see (Black)) is even simpler than for cash instruments which sustain financing costs. In the standard Black framework, the dynamics of a forward price is a drift-free geometric Brownian motion (GBM):

$$\frac{dF_t}{F_t} = \sigma dB_t \tag{9.1}$$

where t denotes time and B_t standard Brownian motion.

This results in a set of option valuation formulas, which are standard Black-Scholes modified for zero carry. For example, the values of a standard European options are given by:

$$C(T,F) = d(T)\left[F\Phi(d_1) - K\Phi(d_2) \right]$$
$$P(T,F) = d(T)\left[K\Phi(-d_2) - F\Phi(-d_1) \right] \tag{9.2}$$

where C and P are values for the European call and put with strike K expiring at time T in the future when the underlying forward price is F. Here:

$$d_{1,2} = \frac{\ln\left(\frac{F}{K}\right) \pm \frac{1}{2}\sigma^2 T}{\sigma\sqrt{T}}$$

where σ is the returns volatility of the forward price and Φ denotes the cumulative distribution function of a standard normal random variable[54]. Note the absence of interest rates anywhere other than in the discount factor to the settlement date, which is a result of the zero-carry attribute of forwards.

All of the action in these pricing formulas is in the volatility σ. Everything else is known from either the futures or fixed income markets. When options actively trade, the value of σ consistent with the prevailing price of an option can be computed—this is the implied volatility of the option. Once you have an implied volatility (as well as, of course, a futures price and yield curve), you have what you need to value the standard vanilla options.

The simplicity of this framework is compelling, providing most of what is needed by trading desks with activity confined to standard vanilla options. For those shops whose activities extend beyond vanilla products into more exotic, structured transactions, more sophisticated methods are often developed and deployed. However, even these more sophisticated methods are usually discussed in the context of Black-Scholes, with implied volatilities and various Greeks having nearly identical interpretations.

There are, however, some limitations to the Black framework. The fact that empirical returns show lower volatility at longer tenors (recall Figure 7.4) has modeling implications. It is reasonable to expect lower levels of realized volatility early in the life of an option, and higher levels near expiration. Equivalently, one should experience lower levels of time (theta) decay early

---

54 To get production quality valuation, one needs to modify things slightly for differences between the expiration and settlement dates, but the formulas here suffice for expository purposes.

in the life of an option and higher levels at the end. This behavior is not captured in (9.1) and options with non-standard expiration features or path dependencies require more sophisticated modeling approaches (see (Swindle, 2014) for a more detailed discussion of these issues).

- Comments on Hedging

The valuation framework outlined above is very similar (and in most respects identical) to basic option pricing theory used in other asset classes. The risks and standard hedging protocols are well known. Delta hedging neutralizes the portfolio to leading order price risk. Rebalancing the hedge extracts the extrinsic value of a long option position, and, in the idealized setting of zero transaction costs and continuous rebalancing, replicates the option payoff. For a delta-hedged position the next most relevant risk of an option position arises from changes in the implied volatility—so called vega exposure, the hedging of which requires buying or selling other options to render a portfolio vega neutral.

There are, however, some important facts to keep in mind before rote application of such methods in energy markets.

First, the effectiveness of the delta hedging program implicit in these standard methods can be adversely impacted by limited liquidity in the underlying futures markets. At long tenors individual contracts rarely trade, and a hedger has to choose between paying large bid/offer spreads to get the required hedge in each contract month, or to using liquid seasonal or calendar strips, but achieving only an approximate hedge. In addition, frictions arise due to standard block sizes—trades of 2500 MMBtus/day (1/4 per day) are routine; fractions thereof are harder to accomplish and more expensive. Small options positions can be challenging to hedge purely as a result of this market friction. At the other extreme, large options positions can involve rebalancings that are costly, simply due to large transaction volume relative to available liquidity.

Second, just as stack-and-roll hedging was required to hedge less liquid futures positions, long tenor options positions are often hedged using short tenor options. The result is only a partially hedged position—one with exposure to changes between short and long tenor implied volatilities. In a similar vein, option liquidity is typically highest at or near the money. The fastest way to reduce net vega exposure for a portfolio with OTM options is by using ATM options, but the resulting portfolio remains exposed to skew and, unless properly adjusted, can often yield rough and unpleasant valuation surfaces as expiration approaches.

Finally, there is a fundamental limitation in the natural gas options markets[55]. The most commonly traded options are the monthly futures-based options discussed above, which involve expiration four business days before the delivery month. Options expiring at other times prior to expiration are a rarity, in contrast to other asset classes which offer a spectrum of expiries for a given underlying asset price. The result is a greater reliance on models and more challenging hedging. This issue is explored in much more detail in (Swindle, 2014).

Term Structure of Implied Volatilities

Forward prices at long tenors tend to move less than at short tenors, at least when viewed from a returns perspective. We saw this in Figure 7.4, which showed the systematic decrease of historical volatility as tenor increased. Market participants are well aware of this behavior, so it should come as no surprise that implied volatilities show similar structure.

Figure 9.3 shows the implied volatility by contract on 23Jun2017.

---

55 This limitation is common across energy commodities, including crude oil and natural gas.

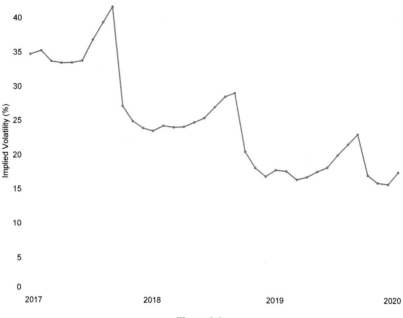

NG ATM Implied Volatilities (6/23/2017)

Figure 9.3

The general decrease of implied volatilities with tenor is clear—options on contracts that have a longer time to expiration usually trade at a lower implied volatility than do comparable options at shorter tenors. Superimposed on this tread are seasonal effects, with winter months having systematically higher implied volatilities than other months. This too is not unreasonable given the nature of winter demand and the resulting high levels of spot price volatility.

We can use the implied volatilities shown in Figure 9.3, in conjunction with the prevailing forward prices, discount factors and (9.2), to value the ATM ($K=F$) options for each contract. Figure 9.4 shows the term structure of forward (undiscounted) value of the calls (or puts, which are the same as ATM calls by put-call parity).

OPTIONS

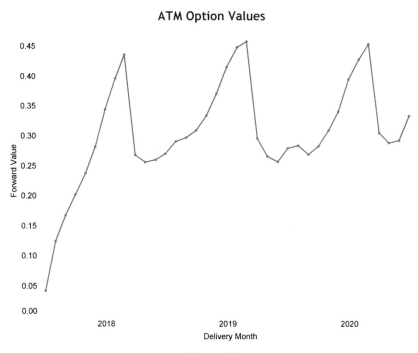

Figure 9.4

Note that the general pattern is increasing option value with tenor, with
seasonal effects superimposed.

A fast way to sanity check option quotes is to use the fact that ATM option
values are proportional to the underlying forward price (just have a look at
(9.2) and notice that all the log terms are zero since $K=F$ so that the entire
expression is proportional to F). If we divide all of the values in Figure 9.4 by
the forward price, we get the result shown in Figure 9.5.

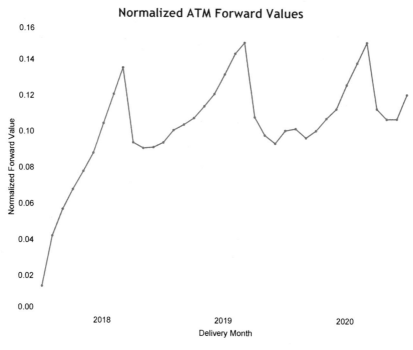

Figure 9.5

The difference between the two previous figures may not seem like much. However, at longer tenors the effective range of the second figure is comparatively narrow. The values of ATM call (or put) options between a year and two years of maturity is 10% to 15% of the underlying forward price, provided that implied volatilities are in the mid to high 20s (which they have been for some time). A simple back-of-the-envelope calculation validates this—if there is a 50% chance of a fluctuation above the strike, and the size of the fluctuation is roughly 25% of the underlying price in one year, then the value of the option should be approximately 12.5% of the underlying.

Implied volatilities are not static. Figure 9.6 shows historical realizations of the ATM implied volatilities of the Jan17 and Jan18 NG contracts. The top plot shows the evolution of each series.

Hedging an options portfolio against such changes in implied volatilities involves constructing a set of options hedges to neutralize vegas—the exposures to the implied volatilities. As touched upon earlier, stack-and-roll tactics are often applied to options positions. The bottom plot in Figure 9.6 scatters the Jan18 implied volatility against that of Jan17. As the Jan17 contract approaches expiration the implied volatility increases and arguably decouples from that of the Jan18 contract. However, well prior to expiration there is clearly a relationship between the two series; one that arguably justifies using the Jan17 contract to reduce vega exposure arising from a Jan18 option position.

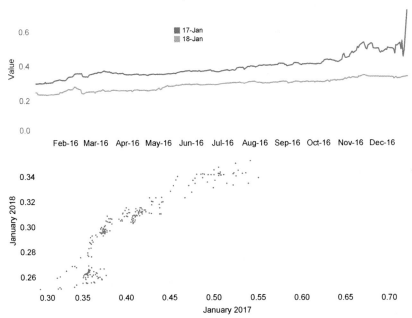

Figure 9.6

Skew

We turn next to how options values depend upon strike. For a given contract month, if the implied volatilities for options at various strikes were the same (a flat volatility surface) the market "believes" that the GBM model (9.1) shown earlier is an accurate representation of forward price dynamics—at least for the contract in question. The natural gas market does not believe this. The perceived risk of options varies by strike, and there is often substantial skew in the volatility surface. In energy markets, particularly natural gas and electricity, prices "spike" upwards. Spot and forward prices can drift downward over long periods of time, and put skew can be observed; however, the most dramatic returns typically result from a confluence of high demand and infrastructure failure.

Figure 9.7 shows Henry Hub spot prices including the infamous polar vortex winter. These are spot prices far south near the Gulf; the nearby forward contracts behaved similarly. In the northeast, price dynamics was even more dramatic.

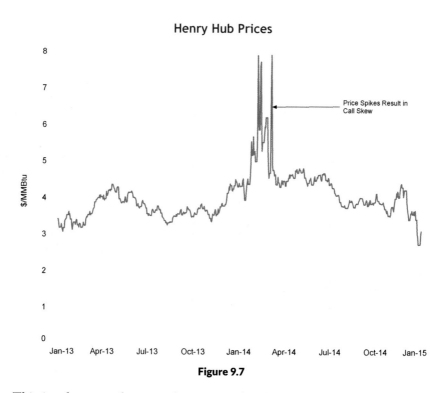

Figure 9.7

This is why natural gas markets are inclined toward call skew—relatively expensive OTM calls at high strikes versus comparable OTM puts at low strikes.

Figure 9.8 shows the implied volatility for delivery months in the injection and withdrawal seasons (Jan2018 and Jul2018) as a function of price ratio—the ratio of the strike of the option to the prevailing forward price. Strikes with a price ratio greater than one correspond to OTM calls; price ratios less than one to OTM puts[56].

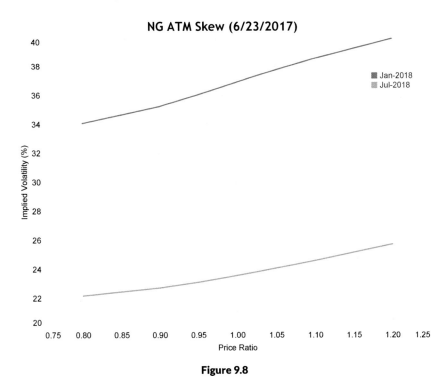

Figure 9.8

Both contracts show the expected call skew, but the summer contract shows both lower implied volatility levels and a lower skew (at least in absolute terms) relative to the winter contract, which traders universally view as a more "dangerous" month.

Just how concerned market participants are of price spikes evolves over time. In the current environment with shale gas production surplus pushing prices down and reducing the fear of shortages, options traders are rela-

---

56 Price ratio is one way to parameterize moneyness of options; its virtue is its simplicity and ease of interpretation. Many practitioners prefer other metrics such as option delta, which effectively controls the range of the parameterization and which scales naturally with volatility.

tively sanguine about high volatility events. In fact, the pre-shale natural gas volatility surfaces showed much more pronounced call skew than is seen at present. The dynamics of forward prices has indeed been changing. Figure 9.9 shows the evolution of a measure of how non-normal forward price returns have been. Here the rolling first nearby returns were analyzed over a ten year period. Each bar shows a distance from normality (referred to as the Kolmogorff-Smirnov distance) that historical returns exhibited over the preceding two years.

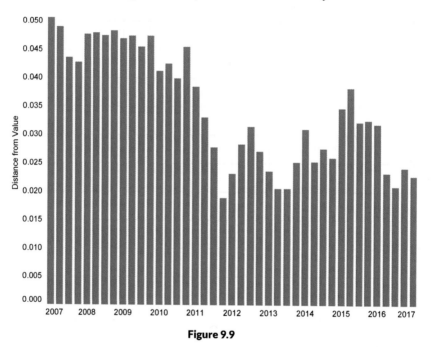

Figure 9.9

The unit of the y-axis has a precise mathematical interpretation, but the purpose of this figure is to show the rather noteworthy drop in non-normality of returns, with a transient increase circa 2015 due to polar vortex effects. This change is likely the result of the shale gas glut. At least for now, natural gas prices are viewed as relatively tame.

Commercial Applications and Common Structures

Why are options traded? As we mentioned at the start, optionality embedded in physical assets motivates options hedging activity. Often, however, options are simply a vehicle for constructing speculative trades of various sorts. We conclude this chapter by discussing various situations in which options trading arises.

- Directional Bets

Traders often use options to express a view, a euphemism for speculation, both on underlying spot or futures prices, and on option prices directly.

On 06/23/2017 the Jan18 futures contract settled at $3.294. Suppose that, for whatever reason, you believe that the price will expire above $4.00. One way to reflect this view is to buy the futures contract. The simplicity of this approach is compelling, but it leaves you unprotected should prices fall; your exposure to price drops is essentially unlimited[57]. Alternatively, you can consider buying a call option struck at say $3.50. The market price of the call on this date was approximately $0.27; the ATM implied volatility being 0.38 (38%). If you buy the call at this price, to break-even by option expiry on 12/26/2017, the Jan18 price would need to settle above $3.77. If in fact your view was correct, that is if the price at expiration exceeds $4.00, you will make at least $0.23. All of these values are in $/MMBtu, and can appear trivially small. Remember, however, that one contract (a very small position) multiplies all values by 10,000.

Options can also be used to speculate on option values (equivalently implied volatilities) directly. If you believe, again for whatever reason, that Jan18 implied volatility of .38 is higher than it "should be", you could sell an ATM

---

[57] Price is presumably bounded below by zero, but this is rarely a price floor of practical consideration. You would likely have unwound your trade to reduce further losses, or been shut down by your management long before the price hits zero.

option. Since this view of yours is about implied volatilities, you presumably do not want to have a position in the underlying forward price[58]. As a consequence, you would delta hedge whatever ATM option you sold. In this situation it is more efficient, however, to sell a straddle (equal notional of ATM puts and calls). You would then delta hedge the short option position.

Relative value trades between distinct options are also common. A long or short option position in one contract month is traded against an offsetting position in another contract month or commodity. Such option spreads can be between options on distinct natural gas futures contracts, thereby taking a position on the term structure of implied volatility; between distinct strikes on the same contract, which has skew exposure; or as a spread between a natural gas option and an option position in a related market, most commonly electricity, in so-called cross-commodity volatility trading.

- Hedging Price Exposure

Options structures are commonly used to hedge price exposure to the underlying futures contracts. Producers of natural gas need to be able to sell what they produce at a price that is high enough to cover their costs. These costs include not only the variable production costs (wages, equipment, insurance and the like), but also costs associated with servicing whatever debt was incurred in the entire process of exploration, land acquisition and production. This means that at some price level debt can no longer be serviced. Variable costs can be dialed down, by slowing or stopping production, perhaps with degradation of the future productivity of the well. But other costs, such as debt servicing, simply must be covered to avoid default. This motivates the idea of using puts with strikes set at the critical price level where things go wrong. Purchasing a strip of monthly put options with strikes and

---

58 If you also had a view on the direction of the Jan18 futures price, this should be reflected in a separate trade so that you can track the performance of distinct trading strategies..

notional amounts set so as to support debt service and operations at all price levels can ensure survival of the business.

Of course, you don't get the put options for free, and the premium that would be required is often too high to fund up-front. This motivates a structure called a "costless collar" in which the hedger funds the purchase of the desired puts by selling out-of-the money (OTM) calls. The hedger receives the payoff shown in Figure 9.10. The swap payoff is shown for reference.

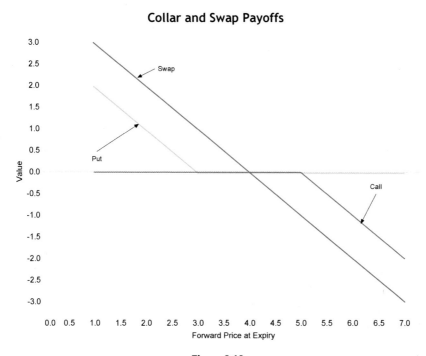

Figure 9.10

Note that when viewed from the dealer's (the hedge provider's) perspective, the structure is the same as the collar shown in Figure 9.1. The dealer is providing the hedger with the put, which insulates the hedger against price drops. In return the dealer receives the call option.

Typically the strikes are set so that no premium is required, thereby earning the name "costless collars." When the strikes are identical the collar becomes a simple swap. Costless collars can, therefore, be viewed as relatively simple extensions of swaps—in both cases no premium is exchanged up front. This does not mean that the structures are truly costless; the strikes are usually set so that the trade has positive initial value for the dealer. One way or another, the hedger pays for the hedge, and in this case the cost is embedded in the structure.

- Hedges with Embedded Speculative Positions

Hedgers do not always like the market price. Producers often have a bullish bias, viewing prevailing market prices as low relative to what they "should be". Nonetheless, investors expect to see future production hedged to some degree. A quandary arises—producers who believe that prices are going to rise are disinclined to lock in future sales at current forward prices. Dealers, of course, are quick to provide solutions. Here are two examples.

The "knock-out" structure was popular in the years preceding the credit crisis. In this structure the dealer agrees to purchase natural gas at an above market price—the bullish producer is happy. In return, the hedge protection vanishes ("knocks out") at a certain price level[59]. Figure 9.11 shows this structure.

59 The term "knock-out" in this context refers to a European feature. This is confusing as in other asset classes the term is more commonly used in the path-dependent sense.

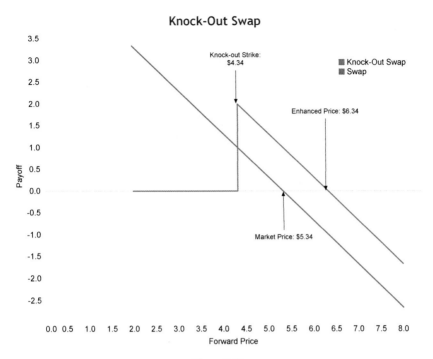

Figure 9.11

The producer gets to announce to the world that future production has been sold at above market prices, caveated by the fact (often less enthusiastically announced) that downside price risk has been hedged only insofar as prices do not drop too much. If, however, prices do fall below the knock-out level, the producer is completely unhedged. This is clearly a "bullish" hedge—a term that is certainly something of an oxymoron.

Everything goes well unless a price collapse occurs, as it did in 2008, resulting in considerable carnage among those who adopted such hedging strategies. Along the way these structures can cause considerable anxiety, both for the dealers and for the hedgers. Near the knock-out, trivial fluctuations in price can result in huge changes in the value of the trade, and the risk is largely unhedgeable. There is no natural offset to this sort of feature that is purely the construct of commodities structurers.

A few years later, a similar structure called "three-ways" were in vogue. Here, rather than the discontinuous evaporation of the hedge as in the knock-out, the hedge protection ceases to accrue beyond a certain level. Figure 9.12 shows this hedge, which is a standard collar coupled with the dealer receiving a low strike put[60].

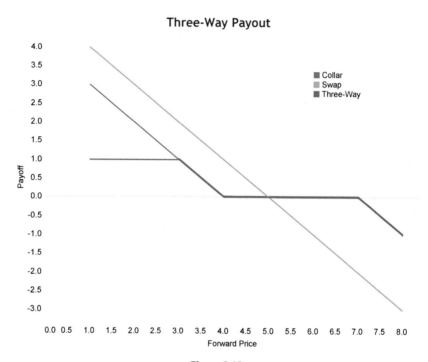

Figure 9.12

- Price Holds

Another class of structures that arise in practice is the "price hold." Large commercial transactions involving project development, financing and associated hedging requirements can have many moving parts, often including contingencies that are hard to predict such as regulatory approval. Nonetheless, in constructing the transaction, firm pricing on the commodity component is often requested, meaning that the hedge provider is asked to hold a firm price on a transaction for some period of time. In doing so the dealer is

---

60 Equivalently, a three-way can also be thought of as a short call and a long put spread.

short an option of sorts. Price holds are usually very challenging to price as they typically involve non-standard option terms.

- Hedging Volumetric Risk

Retailers that provide natural gas to end users are confronted with risks associated with varying consumption. The amount of natural gas used by a customer can vary for many reasons, from changes in commercial activity to family vacations. A primary driver, though, is weather. Homes, stores and factories all use more natural gas on very cold days.

Natural gas retailers are short these random quantities, and high demand is positively correlated with high prices, which can amplify losses. The polar vortex, which produced extremely high demand and prices simultaneously, was an extreme example of this type of risk. Retailers often require more complex option hedges than do producers to hedge these short time-scale risks.

Swing options are intended to help manage volumetric risk. A swing option endows the owner with flexibility on the volume of natural gas received each day during the life of the contract. The general framework of a swing contract involves the buyer purchasing a baseload quantity of gas at a fixed price, with flexibility on the daily delivery volumes. Swing contracts are often defined by maximum and minimum delivery quantities by day, month and for the term of the contract. An example of the key contract terms:

- Delivery period Jan18 to Feb18 at Algonquin City Gate for a fixed price of $10/MMBtu.
- Maximum daily quantity (MDQ): 10,000.
- Maximum monthly quantity (MMQ):100,000.
- Maximum contract quantity: 150,000.
- Minimum contract quantity: 100,000.

The existence of a minimum contract quantity is sometimes referred to as a "take-or-pay" provision, which is to be interpreted as: if you fail to "take" at least 100,000 over the term of this contract, you will "pay" for it anyway. The terms above should be thought of as a contract that allows you to call on 10,000 MMBtus for each of 15 days over the term (maximum contract quantity divided by MDQ); and that you must call on this quantity at least 10 times (minimum contract quantity divided by MDQ). There are also additional monthly constraints that further complicate exercise decisions.

Swing contracts can have seemingly countless additional features which both constrain and enhance the flexibility afforded to the holder of the option, and the analysis of such structures has thrilled quants for years. The challenge in valuation and hedging is due to the fact that the features of these options render them meaningfully different from the most closely related vanilla options. There are, of course, boundary cases where the terms of a swing contract can be structurally identical to a standard daily option, but most transactions are far removed from standard options. An additional complication arises from the fact that physical gas desks will often imbue these structures with additional features that are hard to quantify—risk management considerations intended to minimize the probability of punitive costs ascribed by the local utility should a shop fail to deliver the required quantities at times of peak consumption.

Another class of options used to hedge volumetric risk are dual trigger options—the name arising from the fact that the payoff depends on *both* temperature and spot prices exceeding prescribed thresholds. These are usually financially settling and often take the form of a daily call option on a spot index such as GD, but multiplied by a call option on heating degree days (HDDs).[61] Such structures are designed to provide a high payout to the

---

61 A heating degree day or HDD is defined as $\max[65-T,0]$ where T is the average of the daily high and low temperature at a specified location expressed in degrees Fahrenheit. It is essentially a put option on temperature—colder days produce more HDDs than warmer ones. A cooling degree day (CDD) is a call option of the form: $\max[T-65,0]$. Though unnatural as regression variables, these are industry standards for weather derivatives and exotic structures of this type.

hedger on cold days when the retailer will likely have to procure natural gas in the spot market at high prices to satisfy above normal demand.

As with swing options, valuation and hedging of dual triggers is not straightforward. The dealers that write such hedges, often reinsurers who are accustomed to insuring unhedgable risks, typically use standard futures and options as well as weather derivatives to construct static hedges, inventorying the often considerable residual risks over the life of the transactions.

Regulatory Backdrop

TODAY NATURAL GAS markets in the U.S. are largely deregulated, although there is of course a legal framework that governs the behavior of the market participants. Some entities, such as pipelines and storage operators are heavily regulated. In contrast, the wholesale market, in which participants of all sorts buy, sell and transport natural gas is essentially deregulated. This has not always been the case, and in this section we will survey the key legislative landmarks that collectively resulted in the current market landscape.

The issues confronting the deregulation of natural gas markets are similar to other efforts to facilitate competitive markets when there exists a natural monopoly on critical infrastructure. Rules must be crafted and enforced which guarantee equal access to infrastructure essential to all market participants.

The activities required to provide end users with natural gas can be divided into four categories:

- Production and short-term transport to pipeline networks;
- Transport by pipeline;
- Storage;
- Sale and distribution to end-users.

Of these four activities, production and distribution are suited to a competitive marketplace. Pipelines and storage, on the other hand, constitute the critical infrastructure to which producers and distributors need access, and without which they would not be able to compete. Decoupling transport and storage from other activities is ultimately what was achieved by market deregulation, although the effort took decades.

In what follows we highlight some of the key regulatory landmarks.

Natural Gas Act of 1938

This legislation, sometimes referred to simply as the NGA, regulated the transport rates that *interstate* pipeline companies charge their customers, at that time primarily local distribution companies (LDCs). Prior to this act interstate pipelines had monopolistic pricing power in their respective markets and the LDCs were captive to whatever pricing the pipeline owners were inclined to charge. As this issue related to interstate commerce it was beyond the regulatory reach of individual states. The NGA empowered the Federal Power Commission (FPC) to regulate interstate natural gas transport and sales; LDCs and producers were exempt from this act. The FPC was given oversight of construction and operation of facilities that are used in interstate business, as well as rates charged. The FPC was later transformed into the Federal Energy Regulatory Commission (FERC). (EIA) (NGA).

The Phillips Case of 1954

Producers were exempt from the NGA, and their sales of natural gas to interstate pipeline companies were unregulated (EIA). In the Phillips case [62] of 1954 the U.S. Supreme Court ruled that the sale of natural gas at the wellhead by the producers would fall under the rubric of the NGA. This case had been brought to the court by the state of Wisconsin, which argued that unregulated

---

62 Phillips Petroleum Co. v. Wisconsin (347 U.S. 672)

pricing at the wellhead had resulted in unreasonably high prices for Wisconsin consumers. This ruling in favor of Wisconsin meant that transactions at the wellhead were placed under the regulatory purview of the FPC. The result was effectively a cap on the wellhead price that producers could charge. This cap was arguably too low to be sustainable, limiting the fluctuations in prices required to efficiently balance supply and demand and reducing the incentive of producers to explore and develop new supply. This resulted in a severe shortage at the end of the 1970s. (Nat) (Wisconsin, 1954)

The Natural Gas Policy Act of 1978 (NGPA)

By the late 1970s the flaws of the NGA and related Phillips decision were commonly acknowledged. The Natural Gas Policy Act of 1978 (NGPA) replaced the FPC with the Federal Energy Regulatory Commission (FERC). In addition, the NGPA raised the price caps, thereby increasing the incentives for exploration and production and ultimately alleviating the shortage. It was envisioned that the price caps would be phased out by 1985, at which point wellhead production would be completely deregulated. The NGPA constituted a major step toward a deregulated natural gas market (EIA).

FERC Order No. 436 in 1985

This FERC order transformed the way that interstate pipeline companies do business, affording equitable access to key infrastructure to all market participants. Prior to this order, pipeline companies did not merely transport natural gas; they functioned far more like energy merchants in the modern sense of the term; buying, transporting, storing and selling natural gas to end users. Order 436 required that if a pipeline company offered transport as a stand-alone product, it could not favor its own merchant business over other customers. Caps and floors on transport rates were established via tariffs, and within these bounds the pipelines were free to offer competitive rates to their customers. The effect of Order No. 436 was to enable producers and consumers to transact directly with each other and with other intermediaries on an even playing field with respect to transport and storage (Nat).

Natural Gas Wellhead Decontrol Act of 1989 (NGWDA)

The NGWDA required the removal of all price caps mandated by the NGPA by January 1, 1993 fully deregulating the price of natural gas at the wellhead. NGWDA also required the removal of all price ceilings dictated by the Natural Gas Policy Act of 1978 (NGPA) by January 1, 1993 ((EIA)).

Clean Air Act Amendments of 1990 (CAAA)

CAAA introduced several programs for the purpose of improving air quality, imposing restrictions on the release of pollutants into the atmosphere. By promoting cleaner burning fuels, the CAAA helped to stimulate the increased usage of natural gas in electricity generation.

FERC Order 636 of 1992

This order required that pipeline companies completely separate their pipeline transport businesses from any merchant energy activities. Pipeline companies could no longer offer bundled services, which helped to ensure that other market participants could acquire transport on the same economic terms as affiliates of the pipeline. Order 636 also required that pipeline companies offer storage capacity, increased flexibility in receipt and delivery points. Moreover, the order mandated capacity release programs which allowed customers to trade transport and storage capacity. Finally, Order 636 required that pipeline companies provide all shippers with access to important information in an equitable and timely fashion. This resulted in the creation of Electronic Bulletin Boards (EBB) for the dissemination of relevant operational information of capacity offerings (FERC) (Nat).

Energy Policy Act of 1992 (EPACT)

EPACT provided the foundation for the wholesale electricity market, which due to significant and growing natural generation capacity, affected natural gas markets also. The EPACT established a new category of electricity producer, the exempt wholesale generator (EWG). EWGs were not subject to the constraints on non-utility electricity generation specified in the Public Utility Holding Company Act, making it easier for them to enter the wholesale electricity market. The law also mandated that the FERC ensure access to the national electricity transmission system for wholesale suppliers on a case-by-case basis. These provisions effectively freed utility-affiliated and nonaffiliated power producers to build non-rate-based power plants, a paradigm under which a great deal of natural gas-fired generation was built.

Dodd-Frank Act

Among the many consequences of the credit crisis of 2008 was the passage of the Dodd-Frank Act and the associated Volker Rule. Although little, if any evidence suggests that commodities markets were in any way causally related to the credit crisis, commodities were a major focus of the regulatory aftermath. Dodd-Frank empowered the CFTC to enhance regulation of futures and closely related OTC swaps markets. The details of the implementation of Dodd-Frank continues to evolve, with increased uncertainty as a result of the 2016 elections. While the future of these regulations is unclear, they did provide a significant impetus for the decrease in bank presence in commodities trading, in addition to precipitating a dramatic increase in exchange cleared transactions with a commensurate drop in bilateral OTC transactions. These are ostensibly stabilizing influences in that credit risk is now more concentrated in futures exchanges.

LNG Exports

The increase in shale gas production and the precipitous drop in natural gas prices in North America has spawned the development of LNG export facilities. Import and export of natural gas is regulated under the Natural Gas Act of 1938 and any such action must be approved by the DOE and the FERC, which collectively review and approve applications in the light of whether or not the proposed export is consistent with the public interest, in addition to regulating the siting and construction of LNG facilities (NGA).

BIBLIOGRAPHY

(Black) F. Black, *The pricing of commodity contracts.* Journal of Financial Economics, 3(1):167-179, 1976.

(BP) British Petroleum. 2017. *Statistical Review of World Energy.* 2017.

(Economist, 2017) The Economist, May 20th-26th, 2017 pp. 63-64.

(EIA) Energy Information Administration. Energy Information Administration (EIA). [Online] www.eia.gov.

(IEA, 2016) Electricity Information (2016 Edition): International Energy Agency, 2016.

(Eydeland et al., 2003) A. Eydeland and K. Wolyniec. *Energy and Power Risk Management: New Developments in Modeling, Pricing and Hedging. Wiley & Sons, Hoboken, NJ.*

(FERC) *Federal Energy Regulatory Commision (FERC).* [Online] www.ferc.gov.

(FERC, 2011) Federal Energy Regulatory Commission. 2011. *Technical Report.* 2011.

(Foss, 2012) Michelle Michot Foss, Introduction to LNG, An overview on liquefied natural gas (LNG), its properties, the LNG industry, and safety considerations. Center for Energy Economics, The University of Texas, Austin. June, 2012.

(NAT) Natural Gas Supply Association (NGSA). [Online} www.naturalgas. org. Natural Gas Act of 1938.

(O'Reilley, 2011) *Industry Survey: Chemicals.* s.l. : Standard and Poor, 2011.

(Platts, 2014) July 7, 2014, Platts, Natural Gas Daily.

(Swindle, 2014) *Glen Swindle, Valuation and Risk Management in Energy Markets,* Cambridge University Press, New York, NY.

(Wisconsin, 1954) *Phillips Petroleum Co. v. Wisconsin.* 347 U.S. 672, 1954.

INDEX

Made in United States
Orlando, FL
22 February 2023